just one more drive

just one more drive

The true story of a stuttering homosexual and his race car

Robert James O'Brien

TIDEWATER
PRESS

Published by Tidewater Press
New Westminster, BC, Canada
www.tidewaterpress.ca

ISBN 978-1-7751659-4-1 (paperback)
ISBN 978-1-7751659-5-8 (html)

Cataloguing in Publication Data available from Library and Archives Canada

Cover design: Kiri Northam
Author photo: Mark Brennan Photography

NOTE: Some names and identifying details have been changed to protect the privacy of individuals and groups.

3 5 7 9 10 8 6 4

Printed in Canada

For Nana (Margaret) O'Brien, my number one fan. Without your love and support throughout the years, this book would never have seen the light of day, and I would not be the man I am now. Thank you from the bottom of my heart.

Contents

Preface

The power of story should never be underestimated, because we are the sum of the stories we tell ourselves. As a child, I told myself amazing stories. Stories of fast cars, starships and transforming alien robots. I would sit for hours in the driver's seat of my dad's car imagining my life as a grown man when I could drive for myself; when I would be married and successful and happy. That was before I learned that having a stutter was an affliction and being gay was a curse and the life I imagined would never be mine. After three and a half decades of hard work and struggle, I was sitting in my father's M3, affectionately called the Beast, facing up to an unsuccessful suicide attempt. With nowhere to go, I had to begin telling myself a new story, and this book is the product of that tale.

This isn't a book about recovering from a stutter or a gay coming-of-age tale. It is a story about faith and love and how my bond with a race car helped me to reclaim everything that I thought I had lost as an innocent child. This bond, on that day, saved me and I was determined to honour it by living the life I would choose for myself. A life where I could allow myself to stutter and be gay because they are both a part of me. A life where I could love and be loved in return in the arms of a man, because we all deserve that basic human connection. A life where I could feel the joy of just one more drive, because driving is what feeds my soul and this M3 is the queen of my heart, then, now and until I draw my last breath.

This is our story.

December 2013 I love my M3, I really do, but today our twenty-year relationship is being tested and the Beast is letting me down. The engine has been running for more than five minutes and I'm still not dead. Far from it. The M3's engine, famous for its rough, racing-derived heart, is doing its best to shake me and the car apart even at idling speed. Revving only makes things worse and I'm revving it hard in a futile attempt to fill an aircraft hangar with enough carbon monoxide to kill myself.

The engine's lack of refinement, however, is the least of my suicidal concerns: this hangar is huge. It's all Dad's fault. He had to build a bloody aircraft hangar at the back of his garden rather than a garage like any normal person. Forget his helicopter, this hangar could accommodate a small fleet of flying machines, which means my battle with life is not going well.

Here are the facts: the M3's fuel tank holds 60 litres of unleaded fuel. Of course I know this—I am a car nerd. The red needle indicator on the fuel gauge is telling me there are only 20 litres left, and the idling engine shakes the car, making it feel like the Beast is laughing at me. Unfortunately, I didn't have the foresight to bring a hose or duct tape to direct the exhaust fumes efficiently into the M3's interior.

If Colonel Samantha Carter, *Stargate SG-1*'s resident genius, were sitting next to me, she'd see these practicalities as a mathematical equation. "Given the hangar's dimensions and the dispersal rate of carbon monoxide along with the limited fuel supply and the necessary concentration needed to kill a human, I'm sorry, sir, I don't see this working."

Sam would be able to devise a clever television tech-tech solution to make it work, but I know I can't. I reach out, turn the key and kill the engine. In the silence, I begin to laugh. I am laughing because I can't even kill myself properly. I am laughing from embarrassment and from the relief of knowing no one is ever going to know about this. Am I laughing out of relief that I am still here? The tears streaming down my face tell me I'm still alive, and that relief has not been granted by fictional scientists or video games or family or friends or the M3.

I open the car door and step out into the not very thick mist of fumes that waft around me. Opening the hangar door, I watch as they escape out into the crisp country air. Wexford is beautiful in the winter and I can see our family's second home sitting proudly in the centre of the seven-acre site that is my dad's refuge from the world. But I have found neither refuge nor peace here.

It will be dark soon and I am expected home. I resign myself to the fact that I am a thiry-five-year-old, gay, stuttering mess of a man, and that I'm alive.

Still.

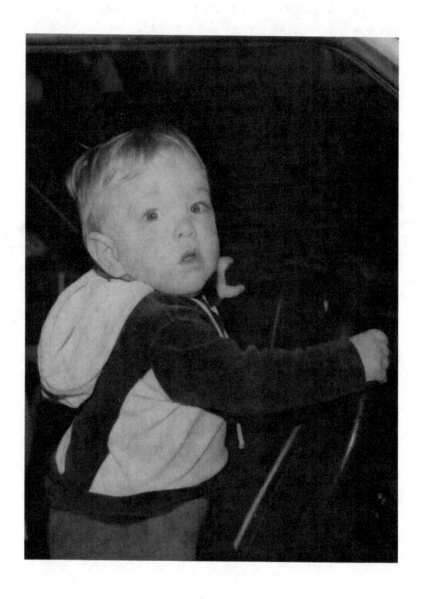

1
Whose car is this, Daddy?

My sister Jennifer once asked me if I was ever really happy. Twenty years ago, it struck me as a frightening question. I thought I had been doing a good job of appearing happy, fooling everyone close to me.

But to answer the question, my happiest memory is when I was seven years old, and my father took me with him to collect his new car. He had owned various cars before this one—I remember an Audi 80 and a BMW E21 3-series. Travelling in these cars soothed me to sleep on many occasions; as a toddler, I would happily make a grab for the steering wheel and imitate my father driving. This new car was something special though. It was the first BMW E30 3-series I'd ever encountered and it would imprint itself on me in ways that would linger into adulthood.

There was no build-up to this memorable day. It was a normal Saturday morning in 1984 and Dad told me we were going for a drive, just the two of us. This on its own was special. I'm sure he had taken me places by myself before, but this was the first time I remember leaving my two younger sisters, Jenny and Susan, behind at home with my mother.

I could sense something was different about my father. He seemed excited and I felt excited too. Growing up, I never saw him get flustered or be overly emotional and, while he was affectionate, he always seemed to me to be slightly guarded. Dad was a self-made man; having grown up as one of sixteen children, he left school at an early age to support his family. He was a salesman by trade and later set up his own business. He has the personality and charisma to sell anything to anyone. He was powerful in my eyes and I worshipped the ground he walked on. I wanted to be just like him when I was older. My father was a man who showed love through actions, not words, and taking me along on this adventure was his way of letting me into his life.

Although it was an adventure, I have no clear recollection of the first part of our journey, how long it took or how we got there. Possibly in my uncle's car? After what I guess was a short drive, we arrived at a rather nondescript house and were greeted by a rather nondescript couple. Yes, my memory is crap at this point, but remember: I was only seven and this adventure was all about the car. It was a cream-coloured E30 320i BMW 3-series, registration TSI-718, sitting in the driveway. The owner handed Dad the keys and I was put in the back seat.

I asked, "Whose car is this, Daddy?"

"This is our new car, Robert," said my father.

That was not really an adequate answer, even for me. So I continued, "But you already have a car."

"Yes, but this one is better," he answered

He was correct, of course—this was a better car compared to his previous E21 model. In a nutshell, the E30 3-series was the second generation 3-series build by BMW in the 1980s. It could trace its lineage directly back to the legendary 2002 of the 1960s that not only helped BMW break into the global car market but cemented their reputation as the builders of the ultimate driving machine. BMW specialized in small saloon cars with large capacity inline six-cylinder engines mated to a rear-wheel-drive chassis with a near perfect 50:50 weight distribution.

This philosophy is what made the E30 such a huge success for BMW. It was a small car but much of its technology had filtered down from the larger 5- and 7-series models in the range.

I was still ignorant of all of this. What I remember most about the car was its interior. As a child of the 1980s, I was fascinated by an American TV show called *Knight Rider* about a man and his talking car called KITT (short for Knight Industries Two Thousand). KITT was advanced in a very '80s kind of way—lots of buttons, flashing lights and a television in the dashboard. A molecular bonded shell made him very strong and his turbo boost feature allowed KITT to jump over things. Total fantasy, I know, but again, I was an impressionable child.

The E30 had some very KITT-like features, including a green LED service indicator that gradually turned amber and finally red to indicate when the car needed a service. The indicator lit up every time the car was started and I always thought the car was happy when it was green and sad if it turned red. Above the rear-view mirror was another LED display, this one displaying service checks. Different LEDs would light up if the car needed water or if a bulb had blown. This was straight out of KITT and for years I looked for this feature in other cars and never found it. Finally, the interior lighting was a soft orange glow as BMW scientists had determined that this was less stressful than other colours such as green or white. Just like KITT! I told myself that this BMW was the kind of car a man drives and was the kind of car I was going to drive when I grew up.

If the interior had won me over, the drive home in TSI-718 cemented my love for it. We spent about an hour cruising through the Dublin Mountains racing on narrow, windy roads. This was the perfect setting for a small rear-wheel-driven car with a moderately powerful engine. I remember sitting unbuckled in the back seat (this being before the time of mandatory child seats), rolling around as Dad tackled the tighter bends, driving fast. I could feel the car slide under me as it broke traction. Dad was laughing and enjoying himself. This was my first experience of a car oversteering; it was fun and probably slightly dangerous too, but I trusted Dad and I trusted the car. I knew we were going to be friends.

After we'd finished driving around the mountains, we had a little chat before going home. Dad explained that no one was allowed to eat or drink in this car, especially children. No one would be allowed to smoke in the car either. Dirty shoes were banned to protect the carpets and seats. Everyone in the family followed these rules to the letter, knowing what a fastidious car-owner my father was. Very few people ever asked to borrow my dad's car, and fewer still were allowed to, which is something that I couldn't understand as a child. My father seemed overly strict to me. Years later, when I asked him why he was so fussy, he explained, "In life you should always treat things with respect. Put your things away, keep your room clean and don't leave a mess."

I suspect growing up in a large family in a small house with very little in the way of material possessions made him that way. I see the wisdom in it now and like to think I have followed his example. Treating things and people with respect says something about you as a person and people really do notice (and judge us) on how we take care of them.

His car was like a physical extension of himself, and my father shared a private connection with his vehicle. I bonded with TSI-718 very quickly and saw it as mine too, if only by association. Every drive was an event and more than that: I felt safe in this car. No one could hurt me and I was free to be driven anywhere. Its innate quality could be felt in the rock-solid construction of the dash, the firm seats that never squeaked and the satisfying thunk the doors made as they shut. TSI-718 felt indestructible.

I can trace this need to feel safe back to my birth. I was born three months' premature and in 1977 neonatal medicine was still developing. At the beginning of my life, I was poked and prodded in an incubator without ever really being held or properly touched. Experts have subsequently told me that this early trauma contributed to my shyness, my stutter and my general unease with the world. Is it true? I don't know, but I do know that the craving to feel safe was first satisfied inside this BMW E30.

2

Hi, I'm Robert and I have two cars

Needing to feel safe was something I learned while in primary school, where I was to discover that life for me was going to be hard. I started my education when I was five at a small, local school run by three old teachers in an ageing community centre. I liked school when I was very small and the smell of wax crayons always takes me back to those happy early days.

Everything changed when I transferred to a much larger single-sex school about a year after Dad had bought TSI-718. I was enrolled in St. Jude's School for Boys for the new term in September 1985, joining other eight-year-olds in third class, taught primarily by Ms McDuff. This was a formal school and I had to wear a uniform for the first time, which I loved; the tie and trouser combination made me feel grown up. On the first day, Dad drove me to St. Jude's front door in TSI-718, with me sitting proudly on the seat behind him.

Initially, everything was great. I was in "big boy" school and Ms McDuff looked like Mum with her short stature and similar hairstyle. I was slightly smaller than most of my classmates and I was naturally quiet. This all-boys school made me nervous, with its focus on sports and competition, neither of which interested me at all. I had just discovered *The Transformers*, a cartoon series about transforming alien robots that could change into vehicles and planes, and this was much more compelling to me than rugby.

The school was run by Catholic priests and they loved me: I

was quiet, obedient and easy to mould and this led to bullying from my classmates. I eventually became known as "teacher's pet." This taunting became worse when I was put in "special" English classes because my reading and writing skills were below average. I began to think that being good was somehow bad, and that I was stupid. Mum eventually got me to admit to bullying after months of misery and she told Ms McDuff, which had disastrous consequences for me. Her response was heavy-handed and bloody insensitive. She dragged me up to the blackboard at the front of the room, turned me to face the class and demanded, "Point out these boys now, Robert! Show me who's been bullying you."

I was mortified, trapped up there with every jeering eye focused on me, daring me to be a snitch. I panicked and did what my first instinct always made me do: obey. I pointed out the guilty parties and the damage was done. What little credibility I had in the class evaporated. I would never, ever fit in, either in the class or the school. My feeling of being a pariah was born that day and has never really left me. Teachers are supposed to plant seeds of learning into their pupils; mine planted a seed that would grow into a stutter.

In Autumn 1986, my parents took action and moved me to a mixed school at the beginning of fourth class. This was a multi-denominational school and far smaller than St. Jude's. Despite my optimism, I couldn't shake the feeling that I had been moved into a smaller and safer school because I couldn't make it with the big boys. At Grange Park School in Ranelagh, I didn't have to wear a uniform and there were both boys *and* girls in the class.

My new teacher, Miss Duncan, seemed nice and in my positive mood I introduced myself to the class telling them about my family, including Mum and Dad's cars.

"I'm Robert O'Brien. I have two sisters, one budgie called Harry and I have two cars."

Later that day Mum collected me and asked, "So what did you tell them, Rob?"

I gave her all my answers, including the two cars comment. "Oh, Rob," she sighed, "People will think you were bragging." So much for the optimistic start.

I didn't understand. Having two cars wasn't bragging; it was just a fact. The cars were as much family as my sisters. But Mum was right. Over the next few days, I heard whispers in the class about "the new boy and his two cars." I was gutted. My first day and the first words out of my mouth had already alienated most of my class. I felt stupid and ashamed. With Dad dropping me off at school and Mum collecting me, these two cars were obvious on a daily basis. I tried to appease my classmates by being as nice as I could be, because I didn't want to be singled out for anything ever again.

Annoyingly, I was also put into another special-needs English class about two weeks after the term began. I had private lessons with an English teacher whose son was in my class, and Dan and I became friends. Dan was very smart and confident—everything I wasn't. In this new school, I began to fear saying my name and I hated reading aloud in class because I felt everyone's eyes on me, judging me and waiting for me to fail. And to make things worse, TSI-718 was about to be replaced.

On a Friday afternoon, Dad took me to Murphy and Gunn, our local BMW dealership in Terenure, which was only a fifteen-minute drive from school. The dealership was huge and airy with large windows and a tiled floor. The dealers' desks lined the back wall and they faced an array of brand new BMWs. I waited by the reception area as Dad and one of the dealers went outside to the service area behind the showroom.

The men wore suits, just like Dad, and they were all well-groomed; some were talking on phones while others were in glass-fronted offices dealing with customers. They all seemed so confident and successful. What an amazing working environment, surrounded by these magnificent cars. I wanted to be like these men when I was grown. In a place like this, I would flourish, not like at school. The dealer Dad had been talking to came back into the reception area to collect me. He was younger than my father, with blond hair and a BMW-branded tie; I wondered what he had done in school to get here.

The service area was even more bustling than the showroom, with mechanics in BMW overalls everywhere. The blond man led me over to a silver E30 3-series, its shape instantly familiar. The engine was being steam-cleaned and Dad emerged from inside the car.

"Well, what do you think?" he asked.

"It's silver," I said.

"I'm thinking of buying it," Dad said, "but don't tell anyone yet as I can't really afford it."

Silver was an unusual colour for a car in those days and I'd never seen an E30 in that shade before. Its front and back spoilers were silver as well and the wheels were classic BBS cross-spoke alloys. Mechanically, this car was identical to TSI-718 with the same small capacity, M20 straight-six engine. But it looked a whole lot sexier and the silver gave this new vehicle real aggression. Two weeks later ZS-4333 was ours.

The teachers at Grange Park and my parents discussed the subject of speech therapy as I was finishing fifth class, my hesitancy and lack of classroom participation having garnered more attention than I liked. Since I was still in primary education, I qualified for state-sponsored speech therapy, which was free but meant a long waiting list. Private speech therapy was and still is the more expensive option. Luckily, we got an initial consultation at the beginning of the summer, just after school had ended. I remember resenting having to go early in the morning for the appointment with a speech therapist. A state-run clinic in Dublin's city centre was the last place I wanted to visit, but going with Mum was easier than it would have been with Dad as I felt less shame over my inability to talk like a normal boy.

My speech therapist was Rachel, a young woman with long frizzy black hair, who assessed me for thirty minutes and recommended treatment: one session every two weeks over the summer holidays. With Rachel, I felt relatively calm, unlike at Satan's Pit, which is what I called school, with my ambivalent teachers and hostile classmates. Rachel encouraged me to slow down my speech and begin breaking up words into their individual syllables. Each day I had to practice a list of one, two and three syllable words. It was embarrassing to do this out loud in anyone's presence, because I felt stupid and slow, another reason for people to single me out and bully me. So I practised in either Mum's or Dad's car where no one could hear me.

That summer Mum took myself and my sisters to a beach resort called Brittas Bay in County Wicklow, so Dad had to drive down from Dublin to collect me and take me to speech therapy. The journey was about an hour and a half each way, and each time we arrived at Rachel's office I didn't want to get out of the car. I wanted to keep driving, driving to anywhere but here. Having Dad take me made me nervous, and I could feel the panic rise in my chest. Rachel invited my father in to see what I should be doing, and I felt so embarrassed sitting there breaking down the sounds in the speech exercises. Dad just sat there in his suit and tie while Rachel coached me. She wanted me to slow down even further and gave me paragraphs to read, in which she'd underlined and marked the syllables she wanted me to stress and elongate.

The session lasted an hour, during which Dad said very little. This was not like him, as he always talked or tried to make a joke out of everything. I assumed he was disappointed by his broken son. Was this how I was going to talk for the rest of my life? I would never be like him, a successful businessman. I would never own a BMW or go anywhere near a BMW dealership or be one of those successful, suit-wearing, confident salesmen.

On our drive back to Wicklow, he said, "You have to do the exercises each day, just like Rachel has said."

"Yes, Daddy. I promise I will."

Dad smiled. "Let's get ice cream."

He let me eat the cone in the car. I was stunned. The no-food-in-the car rule had been strictly enforced for years; this was a big deal for him and I knew it.

Dad and me

After the summer, I joined the sixth class in Grange Park, now one of the senior students. Our classroom was a stage behind the school's gym and our teacher was Ms Butcher, a short woman with short blond hair. She frightened me slightly, as she spoke and acted with more confident aggression than my previous teacher. My private English lessons with Dan's mother had finished at the end of fifth class because my English writing skills were now apparently up to standard. My problem now was the reading. I didn't like reading out loud as it drew the attention of the class. Every time I had to read I would pray, *Please don't let me stutter, please don't let me stutter.*

Rachel's coaching had helped and people noticed my apparent improvement. After reading in class one day, Ms Butcher asked, "Do you find the speech therapy useful? It seems to be working."

Perhaps she thought she was giving me a backhanded compliment. If I'd been an adult, I would have muttered, "Fuck you." But as a twelve-year-old, all I knew was that this was another test. What was the right answer? Beady, judgmental eyes focused on me. So I played nice and said, "Yes."

By this time, I felt inferior to my own siblings as well as my peers. I was the eldest and the only boy, but Jenny and Susan always seemed to outshine me. I wasn't the black sheep of the family, just the broken one. Jenny was amazing, outgoing like Dad with lots of friends in school, never bullied and liked by her teachers. I always felt Jenny was the oldest child, the one to look up to. Today, as a grown woman living in Australia with a husband and two beautiful children, she makes loving and life look easy and I admire her no end.

Susan, on the other hand, was the black sheep. A cute girl who has grown into a beautiful and successful woman, as a child she was off the wall. Her hair was always tied up in some weird bun, her fashion sense was singularly her own, and for a time she went through a self-professed "kleptomaniac phase" in school. She'd show us pencils in the car on the way home, and it wasn't until the school contacted Mum and Dad that they learned that Susan had been stealing the stationery! It turned out that she had swift hands and deep pockets and it took three teachers working in tandem to catch her. She was badass. So badass that a police officer (or Garda as they are called in Ireland) came to the house to give Susan a talking to. I envied her, though. I wished I could be badass, because in my eyes being bad was better than being weak. While I was scared and timid, Susan took what she wanted.

I had no brothers growing up but I did have cousins who are as close to me as brothers. Dean is a year younger than me, has a big heart and is someone who always has your back. Leon is the same age as Jenny and is more outgoing and adventurous. I met Dean when I was seven; Leon was about four at that time. My relationship with them gave me some security as we played video games on their Amiga 500 and watched movies like *The Terminator* and *Róbocop* together.

In 1990, I was a month away from turning thirteen when I started at Zion Secondary School in Rathgar, another mixed school and far bigger than Grange Park Primary. Some of my former classmates, including Dan, were also enrolled in the same school but in a higher education stream, the "A" classes. I was in Mrs. Smithers' 1B2 class with around twenty-five other students. I saw this as a new start and I just wanted to fit in. My strategy was to be as innocuous as possible. I never spoke out loud unless spoken to directly by the teacher and then my answers were as short and stutter-free as possible. It was inevitable that I would eventually be discovered for the stutterer I was.

All of my careful stratagems came crashing down during a music class about two months into our first term. The teacher,

Mr. Lyons decided we needed to learn about brass instruments by reading out aloud about tubas and trombones. As my classmates read one by one, row by row, my heart began to palpitate and sweat beaded on my forehead. My breathing quickened and I felt that blind fear of having all eyes on me when my turn came. I had to open my mouth. I had to read out loud. Anxiety became uncontrolled panic. I couldn't breathe, let alone read. All of Rachel's speech therapy techniques couldn't help me now.

"T-t-t-t-t-t-tubas and t-t-t-t-t-t-trombones are c-c-c-c-classic i-i-instruments."

Painfully, slowly, I managed to get to the end of the paragraph. When I finished, I couldn't lift my head and just stared at the surface of my desk, at the page with all those blocked syllables mocking me. I didn't look up because I knew what I would see: looks of pity, combined with confusion and embarrassment. The room was silent. I could feel my heart still trying to burst its way out of my chest and I was wheezing like a chain smoker on a treadmill.

Poor Mr. Lyons didn't know what to do; some people giggled and others just plain laughed out loud. Any hope I had of being normal among my classmates disappeared before I had come to the end of that stupid paragraph; I was the boy who couldn't read or talk.

Even now I feel a pang of panic when I hear the words tuba or trombone. That memory is as powerful today, decades after the event, as it was in that moment. Stuttering is so much more than a simple difficulty with words, which is all people on the outside can see. The underlying emotions, the fear and panic, are like an iceberg, an analogy many speech therapy organizations use because it is so accurate. I was now too old for state speech therapy and had stopped seeing Rachel. If anyone tried to talk about my stutter, I closed down. I felt like I was being attacked or pressured into more therapy and special classes. The stutter wasn't me—it was triggered by emotions, people and settings. I was nervous all the time, life had no joy and I felt very alone. I didn't know anyone else who stuttered and I felt misunderstood and unfairly ignored by everyone.

3

Are you fucking kidding me! I'm gay as well?

By the second year in Zion Secondary, our class had settled into its established structure. People had their friends and we all knew the social pecking order. For the boys, the boisterous rugby players were at the top of the class, intelligence irrelevant, and they were respected by everyone, even the teachers. I had made a few friends over the year and they were good guys: not sport jocks or extremely popular, just your average second-year students. I felt very lucky to have them.

School became a kind of roulette with my stutter. I would be asked at intervals, usually of around three months or so, to read out loud in class or speak on a topic or say my name. The whole class knew what would happen and any embarrassment they felt was only a fraction of my own. After each speaking event, I would feel traumatized and ashamed and having friends helped. I never completely opened up to any of them as it was too painful. My three buddies, Cain, Eoin and Tim, were the same age as me but they had already hit puberty. Cain had hints of stubble and Tim was proud of his few pubic hairs. I remained prepubescent in every way save for the occasional spot.

By 1991 the E30 generation of 3-series was in the latter phase of its lifecycle and Dad decided it was time to change cars again, climbing up the automotive ladder. Naturally, he chose another E30, this time a 325i model with a larger engine and desirable M-Sport body kit. I had devoured the articles about the 325i in *Car Magazine* and *Autocar*, read the comparison tests that showed how it stacked up against its rivals like the Mercedes Benz 190E, the Audi 90 and the Saab 900 turbo.

Dad's car, the first he ever bought new, was diamond black and everything was colour-coded to match. The M-Sport body kit was very subtle, very aggressive and very powerful. The engine was the same M20 unit tuned to 170 brake horsepower and it was a huge step up for him.

We were to collect the car on a Saturday morning from a dealership on the other side of Dublin. Still a fan of weekend morning cartoons, I was up early and excited, and knocked on Dad's door at about 8:30 am. He was up, in his underwear and doing a happy dance; I swore to myself that I would have more fashionable underwear when I was his age. The drive to the dealership was a long one and, as we crossed Dublin, we talked about ZS-4333.

"This has been a good car and I hope the new owner treats it well," said Dad.

"Are you sad to see it go?" I asked.

"No, it is time for a change."

The Northside dealership was massive compared to Murphy and Gunn in Terenure. BMWs everywhere! Customer parking was to the side of the service area and we pulled in beside an E31 8-series BMW. This was the flagship model in the range and it was the first time I'd seen one outside of a magazine. Dad may have been doing well with his new 325i but it occurred to me that there were men inside who were doing even better.

I was excited and nervous walking into the dealership to meet the man Dad would be doing business with. You had to be a strong man to drive a BMW and strong meant successful and assertive and competent. Everything I wasn't. Everyone around us wore suits and were impeccably groomed—little touches like tie clips and cufflinks. Dad wore suits but never cufflinks. It was as if these suits were the physical manifestation of their status and manhood. I could never be like them and I was feeling like a fraud, like someone who had snuck into a party without an invite. Dad hadn't worn a suit that day and even the soon-to-be-replaced ZS-4333 was looking rather shabby parked beside far superior machines. Then I met Alan.

Dad introduced me to him as his son and Alan shook my hand, saying I could have a look around. Their negotiations went on for ages, while I wandered around the showroom and got to examine every angle of Dad's new car, 91-D-3251, as it sat fresh and clean on the showroom floor. But I wasn't as focused on the car as I expected; something was going on in my gut that I couldn't articulate. Not embarrassment or shame, those were very familiar to me. Was I annoyed that Dad hadn't worn a suit and was making us look bad in Alan's eyes? There was something of a truth there. I kept glancing at Alan and my heart was kind of skipping a beat. I'd never experienced this feeling before and, shockingly, a man was making it happen, not a girl. Cain, Eoin and Tim were always going on about girls but I didn't get the appeal. Yet here was Alan, eliciting this reaction from me.

Lurking around 91-D-3251 was getting boring fast and I felt both terrified and curious at the same time. Curiosity won out; I walked back to Alan's desk and sat beside Dad as the dealing continued.

Alan was tall and had dark hair like Gil Gerard, the actor who starred in the TV sci-fi series *Buck Rogers in the 25th Century*, a favourite of mine. Alan was younger than my father and wore a suit, tie and tie pin. He looked amazing. His hair was neat and combed to the side and he had a clear hint of stubble on his face even though this was early morning and he had probably shaved only a few hours before. I'm sure he had a hairy chest too, but that was not on show. I thought that was manly, like the M-Sport kit on 91-D-3251; hairy men were real men.

What I remember most was his smell. Alan's aftershave was

sweet but masculine and, as it wafted across the desk, the scent offered a teasing hint of what might lie beneath. I forgot about the cars. I forgot about Dad. All I could do was sit there in silence gawking at Alan, no idea what to do or say. Thankfully, he was more focused on the car deal than on the awkward foureen-year-old who was feeling emotions of sexual excitement for the first time. This caught me off guard, yet it probably shouldn't have. Buck Rogers had sexy space princesses and women fighter pilots who had never loaded my torpedo tubes or spooled my hyper-drive in any way. I had always assumed that my focus on Buck Rogers the man was a kind of hero worship. While I was sitting arm's length away from Buck's very real and wonderfully smelling doppelgänger, I knew there was something more going on. I had been so focused on my speech and being invisible that sexuality and physical attraction were unimportant to me—until that moment in the BMW showroom on the north side of Dublin.

I vaguely remember the drive home in 91-D-3251, with the car smelling nearly as good as the dealer. It was immaculately clean and mean-looking with its body kit and alloy wheels, but I was unsettled. The encounter with Alan had left me agitated and con-fused. For the first time in my life, I felt very trapped in the car with my Dad.

As a teenager in secondary school, I was familiar with the term gay. It was thrown around as an insult to disempower anyone on the receiving end. You were called gay if you didn't play sports, or if you showed any emotions that hinted at weakness. Thankfully, I wasn't called gay in school. I was called "Rat Man" by a few of the boys in my class because of my oversized ears. At home, gay was a topic that elicited either sympathy or ignorance. When I was six years old, I met a cousin of my father's, a man who seemed pretty normal to me. He had dark hair in a spiky mullet and wore a leather jacket, but despite his appearance, he seemed kind. On the way home, Dad said to me, "So, Robert. You have just met your first homosexual."

"What is that?" I asked

"It is a man who likes men."

The concept didn't bother me; I accepted what Dad said and didn't feel the need to question it.

His cousin died about ten years later after having a "very hard life." I had nothing against gay people. I was an outsider myself, so I shared some of their perspectives. I just didn't want to be one of them and yet deep down I knew I was.

School was still a rather lonely place, and I certainly wasn't going to tell my parents about the minor name-calling I tolerated. I didn't experience any physical bullying until about halfway through second year when I looked at an older boy in the wrong way. "Germ" was a year older, in third year, but was even smaller than me. One day between classes, as the whole student body shuffled through the corridors, I ended up across from Germ and his class in the crowd. I looked over at him and our eyes locked. Eye contact lasted for a second too long and I saw his whole demeanour change. My look hadn't been challenging or sexual in any way, but Germ saw something in it. I thought nothing more of the incident until the following week when our paths crossed at the same time and along the same corridor. As we walked past each other he pushed me. I stumbled but didn't fall. Germ sneered at me. For months I avoided that corridor and went another way to class. Now I had to be on guard whenever I was on my own at school. Cain, Eoin, Tim and I usually travelled in a pack but there were always times when I was vulnerable. It was just another thing to deal with.

In third year, I sat the Junior Certificate, my first state exam, along with the rest of my class. Everyone expected my performance to be low to average, but in the end I got a very respectable score. Nothing outstanding, but on par with everyone else. Fourth year, in 1993, was transition year, and the classes were split up into streams and disbanded. For me, this meant that my friendships began to break apart. Cain, Tim and Eoin began dating various girls in our group while I survived on the fringes. I liked the girls in our classes and gravitated towards them, but they were never sexual objects to me. Who I was beginning to notice were Cain and Tim. They had stubble now and, when we were in the changing rooms, I saw wisps of chest hair too. I didn't know how to deal with what I was feeling, which reminded me of Alan, and that was dangerous. Too dangerous to stay their friend, and so I purposely drifted apart from them.

Sex and sexuality were becoming more of an issue for me. We had a class called "Education for Living," in which very little relating to emotions or sexual health was touched on, and nothing about sexual orientation or preferences. The course was designed to leave us ignorant and ill-equipped. Our teacher was a rather uptight, middle-aged woman who instructed us on useless hygiene issues like washing, grooming and shaving. Having a moustache herself, I assumed she knew what she was talking about; it was certainly more impressive than anything I could have grown myself at the time.

Official sex education unsurprisingly taught me nothing. Mum must have sensed my burning curiosity about sexual matters, so she took it upon herself to educate me with a book titled *What Is Happening to My Body?* I asked myself that question when I looked at the front cover and saw a handsome ginger-haired man leaning against a tree. The funny feelings I had felt for Alan, Cain and Tim suddenly erupted from deep inside, terrifying and embarrassing me in equal measure. Thankfully, Mum missed my reaction, as she had simply handed me the book and ran out my bedroom door. I read this book all day, eagerly anticipating the part where it explained about men liking men. Alas, in the end it couldn't explain my fuzzy-wuzzy feelings toward the hot ginger man on the cover. He was dressed in a casual suit and leaning against a tree—I was mesmerized. He seemed nice, educated and somewhat vulnerable just leaning there. I imagined I would feel safe with him, like an older brother, and the whole red-hair thing was incredibly appealing to me too. However, if being gay wasn't in *What Is Happening to My Body?* then it must be wrong to feel that way. I had to keep myself safe, even if I was a sexual deviant or something. Was I the only one who felt this attraction for men? Could a seventeen-year-old boy even be a deviant if he had never had any sexual experiences?

My passion for cars gradually faded somewhat. I had moved on from Buck Rogers to *Star Trek: The Next Generation* and, starships usurped automobiles in my affections to such an extent that I struggle to remember anything about 91-D-3251. I recall my shock and disappointment when it was sold for a SAAB 900, but that car was only a stop gap before the most important car of my life came screaming down the driveway—the M3.

4

Boy meets Beast and is not impressed

The evening Dad arrived home with 90-D-41990 was a typical rainy Irish night. It was dark and I couldn't see the car properly from the window but the outline was clearly that of an E30. It may have looked the part, but it didn't sound right. It was loud, coarse and, to my ear at least, slightly broken. As was his custom to announce his return, Dad revved the engine and it got louder, sounding like a chainsaw, in contrast to the smooth, turbine-like whine of all his previous six-cylinder cars. I was confused and surprised. He hadn't mentioned anything about this car. Why had he kept me out of the loop? Exiting the house only made me more confused. I saw my father, shockingly, sitting on the passenger side! What? Why was he sitting there? Dad motioned me to open the driver's door and take a seat. He was beaming, and I mean one hundred percent glowing with excitement. The dash was typical E30 fare but the car had figure-hugging racing-style seats that clenched me like an unsolicited embrace. There were tacky bright red seatbelts and a dedication plaque on the centre console, describing this car as a "Sport Evolution 1990," build by BMW Motorsport GmbH.

"Well, what do you think?" Dad asked.

"Yeah, it's nice, but why is it left-hand drive?" I asked.

"It's an M3, Robert! The best 3-series there is. They are all left-hand drive," he explained with pride.

"Oh, okay," I said.

"Want to go for a drive?"

Not really. I could see he was excited and didn't want to disappoint him so I nodded in agreement. Dad restarted the engine, which roughly shook the car as it screamed back into life. I missed the Saab.

As we were pulling out of the driveway, Dad informed me that this, the M3, was a homologation special and that BMW had raced them for years with great success. It certainly felt like a race car and in typical Dad fashion, we tore down the road, with a bit of over-steering action as well. We headed for the N81, one of the longest stretches of road around Dublin at the time. As we approached the motorway, Dad accelerated and the buzzing engine noise gradually took on a higher pitch and became a frantic wail as the rev limiter hit 7,000 rpm. I could feel the stability of the car, which seemed to settle as it went faster.

As we got closer to Blessington, the road became a lot narrower and twisty and this is where the newly christened Beast really came to life. The car devoured every bend, with a fluidity to its movements that I had never experienced in any car before. Dad was tittering like a child, telling me between breaths, "the engine is a four-cylinder with a very high rev limit! And the chassis is designed to move like this." He proceeded to throw the car into a bend. I felt the rear end begin to lose traction and rotate, and my stomach lurched just like it did on a rollercoaster. I was clinging to the edge of my seat—there were no grab handles in this M3 (deemed excess weigh by the BMW Motorsport division), so I white-knuckled the grey cloth bolsters on the seat beneath me.

We drove around Dublin for an hour before returning home. I clambered out while Dad walked around his new purchase, stroking it admiringly. Apart from lingering adrenaline and damp patches under my arms, the biggest impression 90-D-41990 made on me was that it smelled like chicken. Maybe that's what burning rubber smells like, I thought. Or perhaps the engine had run out of oil or coolant or something. Secretly, I hoped Dad had broken the Beast so we could give it back.

Alas, no. The car and its engine were in rude health and that was how M3s should be driven, according to my father. The Beast was destined to be an honoured member of the O'Brien family and Dad's pride and joy. Over the next few years, we all began to suspect that he loved the car a little more than any of us, Mum included. He kept 90-D-41990 impeccably clean; fussy before, now he was fanatical.

Every morning on the school run, Jenny, Susan and I were flung around and subjected to bone-rattling journeys. I didn't want any undue attention drawn to me, and this car was not subtle. Imagine the scene: a screeching black car flying up the road to school, piloted by a caffeine-infused, frustrated and usually late father. Me in the front, Jenny and Susan in the back, the three of us gripping our seats, as anything unsecured became a projectile. Dad cursing the "slow brain-dead fools" on the roads who were in "his" way. The Beast would skid to a halt outside Zion Secondary, with Dad stopping only long enough for Susan and me to be ejected from our seats onto the pavement. I would hang my head in shame as the car proceeded to tear up the road again with Dad headed towards Jenny's school. Other students would stare at us, much to my embarrassment. I had been bullied for lesser reasons in the past and I wanted no one to see this car or me getting out of it.

The Beast settled into our family quickly, becoming infamous in the process. One Saturday morning Dad was cruising (his term) towards Meath, taking Jenny and Susan to their horse-riding class. He was running late, so presumably he was "cruising" rapidly down the road. He noticed the Garda traffic patrol car at a checkpoint but kept going. He also noticed the officer get into the car and begin to give chase. Knowing there would be more checkpoints, Dad got off the motorway and spent the next hour "cruising" on back roads, determined to get my sisters to their lesson. The Gardai never caught up with him.

At best, I respected 91-D-41990; at worst, I feared it. I'd heard stories about similar fast, focused cars—Peugeot hatchbacks, for example—that would fling themselves into hedges at the slightest provocation. Or Porsches that tried to kill their drivers at every corner. To look at the Beast was to be intimidated by it and I for one wasn't eager to ever drive this car. When Dad promised that he would keep it for me until I became a man, I felt dread rather than joy.

Beast, Boy, Mum and cousin Dean

In 1995 I was on the verge of adulthood. I survived my years in school by taking it one day at a time and trying to stay invisible. Difficult to do when you sport horrible round Harry Potter glasses, years before J.K. Rowling put pen to paper. Harry's invisibility cloak would have been helpful too, because at eighteen I began to develop severe acne. When most of my peers were past this phase and happily growing full-on beards, I was growing a colony of pustules all over my face. Acne combined with a stutter combined with probable homosexuality made my life tough; I would have welcomed an evil wizard and his minions trying to kill me and put me out of my misery. By this time, I was no longer close with either Cain or Tim. Cain had a new circle of buddies and our friendship withered, but Eoin and I still shared a couple of classes. We spoke at breaks but our friendship was more distant. Academically I was struggling too.

The Leaving Certificate, which is a crucial set of Irish state exams students take at the end of secondary education, was looming and I was unprepared for it, despite studying in my maternal grandparents' home every night. Nana Iremonger was a wonderful cook and her meals alone made the studying bearable. At home, I isolated myself from my family as well. The acne left me on a hair-trigger of anger, coupled with dealing with my stutter and the odd crushes and jealousy I frequently felt towards Jenny's hot jock boyfriends. The only ray of hope in all this quagmire was that I had reached driving age and, for my eighteenth birthday, I was given ten driving lessons. Dad and I had a deal that if I passed my test the first time he would help me buy my first car.

I took to driving like a fish to water. Ironic really, given how disconnected I was from my body. The joy of driving was as much a relief as it was a surprise. To feel the car move and communicate underfoot, and to let my mind and body go and just connect was something I had never experienced before. When the day of my driving test came around, I took the day off school and Mum drove me to the Churchtown School of Motoring. I was nervous but determined to pass; I wanted to drive more than anything else. There was an oral component at the start of the test and my examiner was male, thankfully not a very attractive male, or I would have been even more tense. It was a good speech day, as we recovering stutterers say, and I got through the oral surprisingly well. Then came the practical portion of the test. After driving for forty minutes I returned to the centre; after a seeming eternity in the waiting room, I was told I had passed! I was as ecstatic as a chronically repressed teenager could be. In that moment, I felt totally validated and things were looking up. My family went out for a meal that night and seeing the looks of pride on my parents' faces lifted my heart. Jenny and Susan were happy too, because now they had another taxi driver ready to serve them. The biggest question of the night was, what would I be driving? Dad was true to his word.

"Right, well, Dave Plunkett is selling his Mini," said Dad.

"Great," I said.

"Now it is old and a little worn, but a good first car."

"Right, yeah, ok." Less enthusiasm from me.

"And it's orange."

"It's orange?" I repeated. "I can live with that."

The car could have been any shade under the sun, bar pink, and I would not have cared. 729-UZO was a car, my very own car.

The Leaving Certificate exams came and went over the month of June and I ended up failing Irish, also known as Gaelic. I was not surprised but I was annoyed that I would have to re-take the exams the following year. I enrolled in a private school called Leeson Park in Dublin's city centre and settled into a rather draconian regimen of studying and exam practice. Driving my little orange Mini was the only thing that kept me sane. Having very few friends, I had maintained a constant connection with my cousins over the years and I would frequently drive up to their home and taxi us around the city to shops, cinemas and the like. We were still gamers and usually spent hours playing games like Wipeout and Syndicate Wars on the PlayStation 1 while Dean and Leon's sister Zara got roped into making the cups of tea. This was where I felt most at home while growing up and my first full year of car ownership was highlighted by mundane things. The car never let me down.

I spent most of 1996 studying. When the Leaving Certificate came around again, I passed with considerably higher scores. I had set a goal for myself to get into one of Ireland's premier universities, Trinity College Dublin, which I did, and began studying business and marketing. I felt that by getting into this college I would somehow figure out how to get over my stutter, still a constant presence in my life, to say nothing of my sexuality. College life was demanding, but I was well versed in academic study by this point.

Mum, me and 729-UZ0, the orange Mini

Socially, I was crippled. There were former classmates from Zion Secondary and Leeson College at Trinity, but I avoided them. I avoided the people on my course and dreaded any tutorial where I would have to speak for fear of stuttering and being ostracized yet again. To distract myself, I got a part-time job as a pizza delivery driver.

I was the worst pizza boy. Ever. If you had the misfortune of having me deliver your pizza in Dublin, circa 1997, I know it was cold and missing an order of garlic sauce. I was given a cell phone by the company but my fear of phones, which is common for people with stutters, meant I spent a lot of time lost in the city in a panic. The fact I never crashed or killed anyone amazes me to this day. But I did nearly run a police car off the road one Saturday night in Donnybrook village. I was heading back to the pizza restaurant and, not concentrating, I cut off a car in the outside lane. They honked at me and I flashed my hazard lights as an apology. The vehicle honked again and this time the honk was accompanied by a siren and red and blue flashing lights. They pulled me over and two Gardai emerged from the car. I was freaking out and sweating like a prostitute in a confessional. *What if I stutter, or they arrest me, or something worse? I won't survive prison! I could get ass raped! Shit, what if I enjoyed it?*

The two Gardai, a man and woman came up either side of 729-UZO. The female Garda was not happy. She tore strips off me while I fought back tears. Her partner came around to the driver's side, stated that everything about the car was in order and asked me what I was doing. I blurted out that I was a lost pizza delivery boy and that I normally drove wonderfully. My panic turned to something rather more sexual when I looked at his face. *He's got amazing eyes.* I stopped talking. Then I noticed how his uniform was filled out rather nicely and that he had handcuffs. These, I discovered, are a turn-on. I was in the presence of an attractive man,

a "Hot Cop" and those fuzzy-wuzzy feelings reappeared unexpect-
edly. Here I was, pushing twenty, and the last time I had felt them
so powerfully was in a BMW dealership intoxicated by Alan's
aftershave. The female guard spoke up and broke our awkward
one-sided sexually charged moment. She barked a warning to pay
better attention next time. Hot Cop nodded at me in agreement,
broke eye contact and walked back towards their patrol car.

I sat in the Mini for a few minutes after they had left; I wasn't
concerned about my driving but engrossed in the feelings stirred
in me by the Hot Cop. I wanted to see him naked, I wanted to
touch him and I wanted to be held by him. I wanted to deny those
feelings, but they were so powerful that I was happy to be able to
feel such sexual feelings; part of me wanted more, but that would
mean admitting to myself that I was gay and I wasn't willing to
accept that. I convinced myself that I could suppress these feelings,
keep driving, studying and pretending that everything was fine.

729-UZO was my lifeline but its days were numbered.
Mechanically and structurally it was showing its twenty-plus
years of life on the road. It began to overheat and groan with
increased frequency and on one occasion I feared it would burst
into flames with Dean, Leon and me onboard. I pulled the Mini
over and Leon and I jumped out, running for our lives, leaving
Dean stuck in the back of the car. It didn't explode but died on
the side of the road.

The orange Mini wasn't the only fatality that year. My primary
school friend Dan committed suicide and his death hit me hard.
We hadn't been close for years, even though he'd been at Zion
Secondary and Trinity. He was incredibly clever, unlike me, but
socially awkward, just like me. No one could understand why he
had done it. No one, except me. Living with the embarrassment
of my acne, the fear of my stutter and my denied sexuality, I was

5

No fairy tale, no ginger prince

On October 17, 1998, I turned twenty-one. I was disappointed with my life. Having reached adulthood, I still hadn't magically figured everything out. While watching an episode of *Star Trek: Voyager* with Dean and Leon, I pondered what I had done wrong. Like that starship's resident cyborg, Seven of Nine, I found myself struggling with my emotions. I wanted to feel happy, or at least content. My acne had gotten worse and I had been wearing braces for about six months, having decided to get them after years of being self-conscious about my teeth. Looking at myself in the mirror, I saw nothing manly.

The Mini hadn't actually died, but its water pump had. I was expecting it back on this auspicious day, so imagine my surprise when a scruffy looking Mk 2 Volkswagen Golf arrived in the driveway. Dad emerged from the car.

"Happy Birthday, son! Come on, give it a go," he urged.

I looked the car over: it was tatty, with holes in the dash and a persistent musty smell. When I tried to start the engine, it stalled and needed a push to get going again. We drove it around the block, and it did feel more solid than the Mini.

"It will scrub up well," Dad said. "Don't worry. We can sell the Mini to help cover the cost."

I nodded in agreement and thanked my father.

When we returned home, I turned into the driveway. There, surrounded by friends and family, was 88-MO-2911. This other Golf, a shiny black Mk 2, was the prototype *Excelsior* to the battered *Enterprise* from *Star Trek 3: The Search for Spock*—clean and factory fresh. I turned to Dad, who burst out laughing then hugged me.

"Happy Birthday, Rob," he said.

The black Golf was gleaming and looked like a real GTI; it was, in fact, a base 1.3-litre, 55bhp Golf. But the exterior looked authentic with the correct front spoiler and grill. The wheels were the same fifteen-inch cross-spoke wheels that had served 91-D-3251! Dad had kept them and spent weeks looking for the VW roundels to place in the centre of the wheel hubs. The interior was the genuine article, too: sourced from an enthusiast and pristine.

Was this car going to usher me into manhood? I know it was a sign of love from the people closest to me but I didn't feel I deserved it. If they really knew who and what I was, would they still love me? The Mini was sold a few weeks later, with Dad taking care of the sale because I deliberately left it to him. I wanted to wash the old car away and with it myself. I wanted to start again and pretend everything was fine. The truth was I was terrified to step up and sell my own car, to use the phone, to face people. I knew that, as amazing as this new car was, 88-MO-2911 wasn't going to change me.

I had always been close to my grandparents, on both sides, and would frequently visit them once I had begun driving. The day after the reveal of my birthday car, my mother's parents paid us a visit to see me and 88-MO-2911. This was particularly memorable, because it was the day my grandfather bought me my first official pint of beer. A good boy, I had taken "the pledge" years before, which was a promise not to drink until I was twenty-one. The reality about me and alcohol was that I was afraid to ask for beer in a pub or bar in case I stuttered; and if I did get drunk, I might out myself as gay. It was easier to abstain, so the pledge had been no burden for me.

Grandad, Nana, me and the Golf

Granddad buying me my first pint was special. His taciturn nature meant I could never really tell what he was thinking, but that didn't stop me from feeling relaxed in his presence. Once, when I was about ten, my father had bought me an expensive, all metal BMW model car kit, a racing spec E24 635CSi, with a whole raft of stickers. It was clearly intended for older teenagers and I was finding its construction frustrating. Granddad sat up with me until around 10:30 pm and watched me build it; he didn't help or take control, he just watched. Eventually, he called time and sent me to bed. Only now can I appreciate that quiet support he gave me. Granddad showed me that he had faith in my skills when I had no belief in myself.

Two years after buying me that pint, he got lung cancer and died at the end of a six-month battle with the disease. I was twenty-four, in my final year in Trinity and still driving 88-MO-2911.

This was my first experience of a death in our immediate family. Dad was away on a trip with a group of business partners but managed to make it home for his funeral. Jenny, twenty-one at the time, was in Australia for a year with her then current boyfriend, so she missed both his death and funeral. Mum, Susan, Nana, Mum's two younger sisters and I sat vigil by his bedside for weeks. We all knew what was coming but its inevitability never felt real. I focused on my studies to avoid the feeling of loss; it was more than his death, it was the death of my childhood. Granddad had always been there for me and, as the eldest grandson, I had the longest relationship with him. A week before he died, Mum asked Susan and me to go to him and say our goodbyes. He was unconscious on morphine, and I remember his hand feeling very warm. This was unsettling, because I knew in a few days it would be very cold. What was I meant to say? I didn't want to say goodbye. I wanted to be honest and tell him I was gay, but I couldn't. I thought someone could be listening at the door, or that such shocking news would have him bolt upright in outrage. In the end, I thanked him. "Thank you for loving me and being there when I was building the BMW model when I was ten." I thanked him for being him and I made a promise. "I will be strong for Mum and Nana. I won't forget you, ever." Selfishly, I think I asked, "Please watch over me from time to time, as I may need your support in the coming years."

I wasn't there when he passed away a few days later, but I remember after he died Nana taking me into the kitchen and saying, "He was very proud of you and how eloquent you have become." That moved me to tears. It was easier to talk to him and, if anything, he brought that skill out of me, stutter-free. As I have gotten older, I've grown to respect my Granddad's quiet quality. True communication isn't just talking, it is listening. That is what he did and it was powerful.

When we knew Granddad was not going to see it through the year, Mum sent Susan and me to a counsellor. I resisted these sessions with Mary for weeks; I had been through the wringer with speech therapists and school counsellors and none of them had helped. I didn't want help. I wanted to be left alone. Get my degree, find some job and hope either to get hit by a bus or find someone to miraculously save me, other than professional counsellors.

I vividly remember one of our early sessions during which she asked me about Granddad. Every week she would ask the same stupid question, "How is your Granddad?"

"He's dying," was my response. I was sad and angry for the obvious reasons. But I was also jealous of Granddad. He had lived a good, long life and now it was his time and, like with Dan, I envied him his release. In that particular session, my guard dropped. I was tired, stressed and enduring another acne outbreak. One spot—a huge pustule—pulsed on my cheek, as if ready to burst at any moment.

"Does it hurt?" Mary asked me. I exploded.

"What a stupid question! Of course it hurts! Jesus, of course it hurts, look at it! I have to walk around in public with this on my face! Fuck, I am so sick of this bullshit! You can't do anything for me, I can't get past this, nothing is right. I'm tired. You hear me? I am so bloody tired." I began to cry and then it slipped out, the words I'm sure she was waiting for me to say, "I can't be gay as well. I just can't."

There, the truest, most authentic thing I ever said to her. More importantly, it was the first time I had ever vocalized what I was dealing with inside. She didn't push me further, but maybe she should have. After that outburst, our sessions hit a wall. I shut down once again and made the decision to stop seeing her. It was the wrong choice. Just as we were beginning to make real progress, I was running away.

The truth of the matter was I needed a counsellor. My years in Trinity were not happy or eventful. I got through them by studying and keeping my head down. I had no social life and very few close friends. Having to face the reality of my grandfather's death was like the end of innocence, and embracing my sexuality was something I wasn't willing to do yet. I wanted to avoid the issue.

In spring 2001, I found myself seated at the top of the lecture hall for an advanced marketing class. We had to do a final year group project and unsurprisingly I didn't have a group. I had to put my hand up and admit this to the whole lecture hall. I could feel my acne-ridden face turn an even brighter shade of red and nearly vomited as my legs shook.

"He can be in my group," a loud, confident voice said. It belonged to a man called Keith. I had seen him speak in lectures and tutorials over the year. He was the ringleader of a group of men, all high achievers and he had ginger hair. I would be lying if I said I hadn't admired him from afar, but after my outburst with my counsellor, I had sworn I would never, ever succumb to those feelings again. This guy was eloquent, well-built and a natural leader. Now, he was making me feel safe and welcome in his group and I was both terrified and furious. Furious because I knew this was a temporary thing. His group had been well established for months if not years and I was the blow-in. I was terrified because the feelings I was fighting were going to win eventually. I spent a week with Keith and company working on the project. The use of biometrics in security was divided up amongst us, and I spent the week gathering data. I was elated when Keith said he was impressed with my work. When it came to presenting our project, I had to admit to him and the others that I had a stutter and couldn't participate. Keith and one other man, I don't remember his name, presented our project to the lecture hall the following week; I sat both in awe of their power and eloquence and bitter disappointment at not being able to take part. I couldn't risk stuttering and breaking down in front of all these people, especially Keith, but the same boy inside of me wanted to give it a try—to dance metaphorically with Keith on stage and present the project as his equal. That dream lasted for an hour. After the lecture, our project was complete and the group disbanded. I never got to work with them again. When we passed each other in the halls, we would nod and say hello, but that was it.

Graduation came and went that summer. It had taken me five years rather than four to complete my degree. I had failed statistics in second year and was more than happy to spend another year in university hiding out. My academic marks were good; I had achieved an honours degree along with completing a dissertation on the BMW new Mini launch. I was nearly twenty-five years old and now I had to face the world. My stutter had gotten worse as my anti-social tendencies kept me even more silent and isolated than in primary or secondary school. I was still gay and by now knew it. I had no will or desire to get a job, as the phone would be a huge issue and my inability to function socially would no doubt limit my career.

After years of non-stop studying, I decided to take twelve months off and found a job that got me out of using the phone and closer to cars. I became a car washer for a local rental firm, laughingly just a stone's throw away from Trinity College. The first morning began easily enough: I got to wash cars (and I use the verb loosely) in under five minutes each and got to do it in a shed. My boss had anger issues and shouted a lot but I wasn't bothered because this wasn't going to be my job forever. I was just killing time, recharging my batteries. But after lunch I was sent to the office to make phone calls, specifically to transfer customers' insurance onto our rental cars. As I sat at the desk, facing the files and the phone, my heart was beating rapidly and my breathing was shallow. This was it: a situation I couldn't run from. I hadn't used a phone in months to make a call, let alone a professional one. As any stutterer knows, the phone is our most feared device. You can't hide or use tricks. I was terrified, but I wanted to get through this. I believed that after the first call or two it would get easier. The office was empty, which made it less difficult to pick up the phone. As I dialled the number of the first insurance office, I tried to figure out what I was going to say, what words I could use to form a coherent sentence. The line rang, followed by "Hello, Eagle Crest Insurance."

I got as far as "Hello" before my shallow breathing escalated into hyperventilation. I couldn't talk. I couldn't breathe. The insurance broker on the other end kept saying "Hello" and "Can I help you?" I took the only control I could by hanging up first. Slamming down the phone down, I stood up and tried to breathe.

Why the fuck can't I even make a simple fucking phone call? That fury was quickly joined by self-hate. *Some fucking TCD graduate you are! And you're a bloody total failure! What now genius? Shit!*

I walked out of the office and out the front door, ready to bolt if anyone called after me. I began to jog, then run because I wasn't going back. I ran for as long as I could, slowed and walked with my head down in shame. Four hours later I ended up opposite the entrance of Palmerston Park in Rathgar, about a ten-minute walk from home. I sat on a bench nursing my sore feet, exhausted and ashamed. Running away was something I had always done figuratively, by avoiding situations and people, now I'd done it literally and there would be consequences.

Firstly, I had to go home and face my family. Had the job phoned home? Did they know? I found Mum and Dad in the kitchen and I sheepishly explained what had happened. They were confused and disappointed. I felt like such a pathetic failure and this only reinforced all my beliefs as to why I would never be a success in the real world and was a failure as a man. Secondly, I'd left the Golf parked beside the shed that morning and it was still there. I had to go to pick it up.

As stealthily as I could, I got into the car and turned the key. The Golf wouldn't start and the noise alerted my boss, who was still in the shed even though it was past 7:30 pm. He saw me and confronted me. I apologized and explained that I had a stutter. To my surprise, he didn't fire me and agreed to keep me in the shed just washing cars. I couldn't believe it. I had gotten away with it. I had avoided responsibility and the reality of my stutter just as I had done in school and university.

For months, I stood outside that shed with a bucket and brush, washing endless lines of rapidly returning rental cars. I felt like a fairytale princess trapped in a dungeon, waiting for my prince to arrive and save me. I was so lost, tired and despondent that I had given up on myself and my life. Then one day, a shiny E39 BMW 5-series parked just outside Trinity. This caught my attention. I was transfixed when I saw a handsome ginger-haired man emerge followed by three other familiar looking men. It was Keith and his usual group of friends, but who they were hadn't registered immediately so I didn't try to run and hide. Keith saw me and waved as he entered Trinity; my prince had arrived but had not saved me. I felt embarrassed and very sorry for myself. What were they doing now? Obviously something more productive than me. I remembered being part of that group and the idea of being something in life. I also thought of Keith and ginger hair and what it must be like to be with someone like him. The shed was empty and unusually quiet so I could cry in peace. The reality of my life was hitting home.

Life hit me, again and again, to make sure I was getting the message. 88-MO-2911 was broken into two weeks later, and I knew I was done in the job. Only my radio was taken but still, I had been violated. Then Mum, Nana Iremonger and a family friend called Liam all gave me, within a week, a copy of the same newspaper article about a stuttering recovery program. I took this as a sign and got in touch with the director of the Irish programme via email. I was impressed that email communication was explicitly recommended on the website, and also that a relative could telephone on the applicant's behalf; these people obviously knew about stutterers and their fears. The McGuire Programme was run by recovering stutterers for stutterers; no speech therapists, just people like me. I enrolled in the February four-day course which was three months away, sat idle at home and patiently waited.

6

Pause, breathe, speak and release

The McGuire Programme's four-day intensive course was being held in a hotel in Dublin City Centre. New students, such as myself, had to stay in the hotel for the duration without any contact with the outside world until the final day, which was a Sunday. Mum and Dad were away in Spain for the week so Susan dropped me off at the hotel. She may have been briefed by my parents to stop me running away: she made sure I arrived at the hotel on Wednesday evening at six o'clock, in time for the introduction sessions that night. Susan tried to settle my nerves in the car by pointing out a nice woman on the side of the road sporting a short pink dress and a cigarette dangling out the side of her mouth, suggesting she was on the course too.

"I think she's a prostitute, Susan."

"You are so bloody judgemental!" she shot back.

"Fine, but look, there are lots of nice-looking people checking in," she continued, gesturing toward the hotel's reception desk through the car window. "Look, if it's really bad, call me and I'll come and collect you."

I had been waiting for this for months and so I owed it to myself to at least try. Feeling fragile and teary-eyed, I got out of the car, took my case and waved goodbye.

Resigned, I grabbed my case and walked into the reception. In front of me was a small woman who was breathing rather heavily. Has she been running? I listened to her as she spoke to the receptionist. She started speaking by announcing her name loudly and assertively, still breathing oddly. Maybe she's a bit "special"? To my surprise, other people around me were also breathing in the same way and I began to feel uncomfortable. I heard her say she was in the programme I'd signed up for. These people are freaks, I thought. As the woman walked away, she looked me straight in the eye and nodded with a smile. She wasn't bothered or embarrassed in the least by how she had just spoken, but I was embarrassed for her and all these heavy breathers around me.

Then it was my turn to face the receptionist. In contrast, I couldn't look her in the eye as I tried to get my name out and I kept blocking on the O in O'Brien. I gave up, frustrated, and handed the lady the print out of my check-in letter. She thanked me and told me where my room was. Even in a lobby full of people, who I assumed were recovering stutterers, I was trying and failing to masquerade as a fluent speaker. As I walked up to my room, I considered that maybe breathing funnily (and being at peace with it) along with being able to look someone in the eye was a preferable strategy to deal with my stutter.

This was an adventure of firsts for me: I had never stayed in a hotel without my family before and I would be sharing the room with a stranger, another new male student, as they didn't want anything distracting us. I prayed to any superior power that might listen that I wouldn't be bunking with anyone hot or ginger. That would have tipped me over the precipice I was already dangling above. My roommate, Kian, was a perfectly normal-looking Irish country boy with brown hair and eyes and a head taller than me. He even had a girlfriend. I was too nervous about the introduction session to question him further about his personal life. We talked briefly, and both being covert stutterers (meaning we could hide it most of the time), we also talked rather fluently to each other. He said his stutter had always bothered him; he was in university but I got the impression that it hadn't held him back as much as it had me. Still, it was gratifying to have a partner in recovery that night as we both walked into the introduction session together.

The session was held in a large hall in the hotel that had a small bar attached. The room was packed and this set my nerves off. Who were these people and could they really help? Despite all the research I'd done and positive feedback I'd read, I was still sceptical. I could hear these people breathing, some talking in a controlled, almost robotic fashion, while others were fluent. It was confusing. I got myself a pint of beer, choosing the only brand with a name I could blurt out fluently in the moment. One of the organizers told us to sit with the fifteen or so other new students and wait for the session to start. Now, putting a group of nervous stutterers together at a table with alcohol is a recipe for disaster. Alcohol makes my speech worse while it improves that of others, but we were all stressed. The introductions were a random collection of full names, first names and chronic dysfluent blocks ending in weak smiles and understanding nods of the head.

Strangely, I began to relax. These were people like me, people who couldn't say their names, people who also blocked and cried in sheer frustration. I had always assumed I was the only stuttering person in the world and here, suddenly, was a room full of them. As the clock ticked closer to eight o'clock, more people sauntered into the room. By 8:05pm everyone had taken a seat and Joe, the course director, introduced himself.

He told the new students we were expected to refrain from beer after the session, not phone home and keep an open mind. He spoke in a fluent, albeit controlled manner. He then introduced our course instructor, a tall, rather intimidating man called Matt. Matt spoke with a cool confidence and resonance that made me sit up and focus. Impressionable as I am, I have always been a sucker for powerful role models and I knew instantly that Matt was going to be one of them. He shared his story about his struggles with his stutter. How he, like the rest of us, would avoid words, people and life in general. I didn't quite believe him, but I could relate. He said that he couldn't have succeeded without the aid of his wife and then shared his breaking-point story, which isn't mine to share here but to which I related fully. It was his wake-up call and he explained that it was there and then that he decided to take a proactive step and deal with his speech, eventually becoming a course instructor.

We then heard from an assortment of graduates, some recent, some experienced. They all used a breathing technique that we would be learning the next morning. What struck me were the similarities in everyone's stories. These were people like me, but they were standing up talking and enjoying the experience. They were calm and in control of their speech and I was impatient to see if this technique could work for me.

The social aspect of the programme was, for me, also revolutionary. My experience of traditional speech therapy was being treated like a person with a problem. The expert is there to "fix" you and the whole process felt clinical and segregated. But here were normal people—farmers, bankers, midwives—talking and laughing and just surrendering to the joy of being with others like themselves. The session wrapped up at about 10:30 pm and we were told to go to bed and be ready for four intense days. Not the best way to encourage sleep. First-day videos were on the schedule for the next morning; I was dreading it and consequently didn't sleep much that night.

Day One: Breathing 101

The familiar sound of my phone alarm woke me after what felt like only four hours' sleep. It was early enough, 7:30 am, and I dragged my slightly drunken ass out of the bed. That second pint was the killer! After showering I made my way downstairs to the breakfast room where, under any other circumstances, I would have filled my plate and eaten myself into a food coma. Not today. I knew that Step One on this recovery programme was the first-day video, a recording of you being asked questions. As a covert stutterer, I was adept at hiding my disability by avoiding words and situations but here, now, I couldn't. These people knew all the tricks and I felt beads of sweat form on my brow at the idea of the scrutiny I was going to receive.

After an uncharacteristically light breakfast, I joined all the new students at the front of the room where the video camera was standing, ready for its first victim. Matt, the instructor, asked for volunteers. Another graduate was going to ask us one by one typical questions—your name, address, and so on—simple things. But for us, the simple things cause the most difficulty. I didn't want to be first or last, so I sat and watched the others. It is always difficult to watch stutterers struggle with their speech. I had to stop myself from looking away.

The first person was a tall, middle-aged man who seemed pretty fluent. There were odd fluctuations in his speech but overall, I was suspicious as to what he was really doing here. Another person I remember clearly was a blond woman who had such a severe stutter that she couldn't even get past her name. She began to cry on camera and we all knew what she was feeling. Matt told her to just breathe; as her tears dried, her speech stabilized and she got through it. Kian was the next one up and he was moderate in his speech. I felt my stomach lurch when they asked him to make a phone call. He did, with some stuttering on his name, but to me he seemed almost fluent. Not wanting to lose face, I got up next.

I tried to ignore everything around me and not treat this like a competition. Asked to say my name, I blocked. My breathing was very shallow and I was getting lightheaded. I couldn't get past O'Brien and could hear myself endlessly repeat "em, em, em."

Rage was bubbling close to the surface, making my face burn while I looked everywhere but at my interrogator or the camera. I was losing it. Finally, I managed to get my surname out but the effort had exhausted me and I began to shut down. The graduate asked about my studies and job and what I was doing with my life, but I said very little. The ordeal lasted around four minutes but felt like forty. I skulked back to my seat and concentrated on the floor, avoiding eye contact with everyone in the room. This is the worst part—hold on and see what happens next, I desperately told myself.

By noon all the newcomers had been filmed, and the instructor explained that another video would be shot on Saturday during the "soapbox speeches" and both would be given to us at the end of the course. We broke for lunch and were paired with other graduates. Our directions were to speak only to them and to try to relax. For the second time that day food did nothing to lift my spirits and my conversation with my assigned graduate was brief.

Back in the hall, the chairs were arranged in two rows facing each other. One row was for graduates, the other for new students. After we sat down, we were each given a belt to put around our chest. Matt stood in the centre of the room, also wearing a belt, and said, "This is the most important lesson you will learn today. It is a new way of breathing and it will allow you to control your speech." He was serious about drilling the breathing technique and for the next four to five hours we just sat and learned "costal breathing."

Costal breathing involves using the intercostal muscles by the ribs to drive both the inhale and the exhale phases of a breath. Opera singers and performers breathe from here as it gives their breath range and power. Normal speakers use their crural diaphragm which functions when we take normal, shallower breaths. For stutterers, the dysfluency is in the crural diaphragm:

it spasms when we feel fear or anxiety. So, when we are emotionally triggered, we stutter. This can be caused by a word, person, situation—the triggers are different for each individual. When I was asked my name, the anxiety I associated with that jumped to panic in a second. I could have been talking fluently throughout the conversation, but ask me my name and I would suddenly fall into dysfluency. Costal breathing essentially bypasses the crural diaphragm and gives the stutterer conscious control over their breathing and this requires practice. That was the purpose of the belts around our chests: we could feel our chests expand and relax. At first I felt stupid and slightly lightheaded as I watched and mimicked the graduate sitting opposite me. Having to just breathe and maintain eye contact was an alien experience for me and I was conscious of my acne too, but after an hour it began to feel more natural.

Halfway through this session, graduates stood up to make presentations, providing us with checklists and mantras, all the time using the costal breathing technique. Many of them would also block and stutter, but intentionally, to demonstrate how costal breathing could help. I listened to the graduate facing me and repeated what he said. It was all about drilling the basic technique rather than fully understanding the presentations. Much of the information I heard that day escaped me, but it didn't matter as it was going to be repeated. Today was about breathing, relaxing and focusing.

By seven o'clock it was time for our first test. All the new students had to stand up in front of the room and state their name, address and telephone number while using the new technique we'd been practising all day. Braver men and women than I stared Matt in the eyes and spoke, fluently, calmly and in control, perhaps for the first time in years. It was a transformational hour. The woman sitting opposite to me was the one who had been in front of me at the reception desk when we'd checked in. Diana looked delicate and fragile, but she'd had the strength to get through this process. While I sat there proclaiming that I couldn't do this, Diana told me I could. "Do it, Robert," she coaxed. Without thinking I stood up and locked eyes with Matt. He took a few costal breaths, as did I, then with a deep breath I said, "Robert O'Brien."

My fucking God! Did I just say my whole name?

I took another breath. "47 Park Drive, Ranelagh, Dublin 6."

Okay . . . okay, don't jinx this! Stay focused.

Another breath and with it my phone number. Fluently. No blocks, pauses or filler words. Applause filled the room and Diana smiled at me, but I hardly noticed. Tears welled as I looked at Matt: I hadn't said my name like this in years. While I could be fluent on occasion in the past, for these last few moments I had also been in control and calm as I surrendered to the technique. I was proud of myself. For the first time, I wasn't the victim, a weak pathetic excuse of a man-child.

After everyone spoke, we broke up for the night with a lot of assigned reading of the manual to be done. As I was walking out the room, a graduate came up to me and introduced herself. "Hi, I'm Martha. I just wanted to tell you that you have a beautiful voice." No one had ever told me that before and what's more, I believed her. My mood ecstatic, I studied the manual hungrily back in my room before gradually falling into a restful sleep.

Day Two: Taking to the streets

The second day started with a few hours sitting in rows again, drilling the breathing technique. This was followed by a session in which we began to touch on the emotional and psychological weights we carry as stutterers: shame, fear and self-hate to name some of the more obvious emotions. The difference with the McGuire Programme was that all the people talking about these feelings had lived with them and struggled with them just as I had.

The end of this session was the make-or-break moment. Up to this point, participants could choose to remain or leave. Staying meant paying a fee, which paid for the four full days and after-course support. I'd thrown money at my stutter before, but this time I believed it was worth it. I was staying.

Paired with graduates, we took to the streets of Dublin. The grad's job was to demonstrate the technique in the real world which involved making contacts and disclosures. Contacts meant stopping and talking to people using good, controlled technique. Asking for simple things like directions or the time. Disclosures involved telling random strangers that we were stutterers on a recovery programme and that we were working on our speech.

My graduate was a lovely guy called Brandon. He, like Diana, was a small, rather unassuming individual and, like her, amazed me with his courage and honesty. Brandon showed me that speaking could be fun and that people were supportive more often than not. He stood by the Millennium Spire, the monument erected on O'Connell Street to mark the year 2000, and handed out cards giving information on the programme. He wasn't performing or acting. He was just being himself.

Back at the hotel around six o'clock, we had to report on what we'd seen, done and experienced. Once again, every new student had to stand up and talk in front of the whole room; I was feeling optimistic and excited, which was utterly surprising. When my turn came, I was able to speak without fear and with real feeling, while these people who had been strangers a few days ago listened to and supported me. The warmth I felt condensed and clarified as I sat down: I belonged. I belonged here in this group with these people. This was a revelation.

After our presentations, we had a final breathing session and were assigned more reading. Get a good sleep, we were told, because Saturday was to be a long day starting at 6:30 am with a telephone session. Now, this terrified me more than anything else: telephones were my demons. Graduates would be phoning our room in the morning and we were to answer with our names. No easy "Hello," but my dreaded and often blocked-on name. Kian and I chatted for a while and eventually went to bed. I didn't sleep well. Who would I be if I was no longer a stutterer?

Day Three: Back to Trinity and the soapbox

At 6.00 am I was wide awake and sweating. I'd managed a few hours' sleep, but was certainly deprived of rest. A half an hour later, both Kian and I were sitting by the phone. As was now his custom (knowing it wasn't going to be me), he went first. When the phone rang, he picked it up and spoke his name. Almost instantly after he hung up, the phone rang again. My turn. My heart was pounding and the familiar terror threatened to overtake me. I took a full costal breath before picking up.

Holding the receiver, I found a focal point, took another calm costal breath and said my name, fluently. Some small talk about stuff like how I'd slept followed but I wasn't listening. This was amazing. I wanted to do it again and, for the next forty minutes, Kian and I took turns answering the phone. It was almost like a dance and we were both having fun. This might not seem a big deal to most people, but for me this was my second big victory on the course.

Breakfast was sweet and more substantial, then we took our seats and drilled the breathing technique again for a few hours. This was followed at eleven o'clock by an interactive workshop to practise speaking strategies such as making eye contact, adding music to your voice and so on. It is officially known as the Harrison Workshop, named for John Harrison, another recovering stutterer; it was organized, joyful chaos, like changing up a gear or two in a car. It moved the game along and we began to play with our new breathing and speaking techniques, drilling individual components in an exciting way. I was having fun speaking! Conversation flowed—BMWs and transforming robots, starships and impulse engine manifold designs—anything I fancied. More than just fluent speech, this was the first time I had expressed myself unedited. I could say exactly what I wanted to, and these people didn't care what it was as long as the speaking technique was good.

At one o'clock, more contact sessions on the streets were scheduled, and this time it would be me making them. I was feeling confident but also still fearful. Knowing that I wasn't going to be alone helped, and I was paired with a graduate called Thomas. We walked toward the city centre and I stopped a man to ask him for the time. The first contact out of the way, it became easier as I made more of them. I had a list of things I wanted to do and ask. First stop was a video game store, where I queued up at the counter to ask about the release date of a game. I already knew the answer, but being able to stand in line and not feel frightened was so liberating. Making a disclosure was a challenge still to come. Even though I had seen people's positive responses the day before, my ego was holding me back. The thought of it embarrassed me. I decided to walk into Trinity College and tell one of the campus guards, a woman I had walked past for years without ever speaking to her, that I was a recovering stutterer. She wished me luck although I doubt she recognized me as a former student. My confidence was bolstered even more, but the boost was tinted with regret. What if I had been able to do this years ago?

My assigned goal was to try and make one hundred contacts before our scheduled soapbox speeches on Grafton Street. This sounds like a lot but for a seasoned McGuire graduate it is rather simple. You keep the contacts short and just go for it. I know I didn't reach the goal—it was closer to seventy—but I have since achieved the fabled hundred. Thomas kept count of my contact tally on a little mechanical clicker and after I hit seventy, we decided it was time to eat before the soapbox. We went to Eddie Rockets, a popular American-style diner, where I ordered our meals. Before I'd always ordered coke because it was a word I didn't block on. I hate coke (too much sugar). Strawberry milkshakes, which I love (fruity milky goodness), had been beyond me because I couldn't get the words out. I ordered two strawberry milkshakes. Very small things like these make the most difference and it was amazing.

Most graduates of the McGuire Programme say that the soapbox speeches are what they fear the most. This involves standing on a box on Grafton Street, or whatever the city's main street is, with each graduate taking turns to make a short speech declaring who they are and what they are doing on the McGuire Programme. All the other graduates surround the speaker on the box to give moral support and inform the public about what is going on. Graduates can ask friends and family to come and watch but most people prefer not to as they are already nervous enough. The soapbox speeches are also recorded and are the second video that every graduate receives. After facing the phone and disclosures and the guard in Trinity, I was ready for this. The day had been a culmination of successes and this public proclamation was going to be my final rite of passage, one I was excited to embrace. I took my turn in line behind other fellow new graduates behind the old Dunnes Stores on Grafton Street, the main shopping street in Dublin which is always crowded. I began with my name and address, just as I had done on the first night, then I declared I was on the McGuire Programme, a recovery programme for stutterers and thanked all the people involved.

Me and the soapbox

Was I perfect? No, I stumbled a little but that was okay. My people surrounded me like a magical ring of protection, while the public clapped and supported all the speakers.

The afternoon was both exhilarating and exhausting. Back at the hotel, we had a split session from seven to nine o'clock, beginning with giving feedback on our contact session. There we all were, breathing and talking when suddenly a phone rang. It could have been the Bat Phone or the President's fabled red phone for the impact it had on us. Everything stopped and there was a curious pause. The regional director answered it, then called out my name. It was for me! Had Mum and Dad died in Spain? What terrible thing had happened? I'd said I'd call them if there was any problem. It was Susan. She was worried I hadn't been in touch and had half-expected me to appear at home. "Susan," I hissed (fluently). "It's okay. I've got to go. Goodbye."

We weren't supposed to take phone calls, and I was furious because I thought I'd be in trouble for breaking the rules. I apologized to the room but no one admonished me as they'd done in school. No one said anything, which surprised me. It was only later that I appreciated the fact that Susan cared enough to call.

Day Four: Endgame

As amazing and intense as the whole experience had been, I was beginning to crack, emotionally and physically exhausted. Kian and I made our early morning phone calls at 6:30 am and the fear I felt the previous day was gone. The full-Irish breakfast seemed just too much after four days, and I was beginning to crave oatmeal. Another breathing drill session was followed by the unimaginatively titled Going Home session. The programme fee included after-course support, which consisted of a speech coach who you were expected to call at least once a week and whenever you were struggling with your speech. We also had access to the phone list, with an international list of graduates and coaches who were free to take calls daily. Finally, we were expected to participate in weekly support meetings and mine would be in the same hotel. This support is vital for successful recovery as the programme doesn't abandon graduates after four intense days.

Family and friends joined us for the final speeches at noon. Jenny and Susan were there as Mum and Dad were still in Spain. Each graduate had a few minutes to stand up and speak about their experience, almost impossible to do briefly as there was so much to process. One guy spoke about how he felt, saying that admitting to being a recovering stutterer was what he imagined coming out must feel like. I squirmed on my seat. There would be a time in the future when I would discover that he was right.

I don't remember my whole speech but I did say that there was nothing wrong with me or anyone of us in attendance that day, fluent or otherwise. Seeing Jenny and Susan crying was a validation; they were two beautiful, capable young women while I was used to feeling like the family freak. Not being the big brother I wished I could have been to either of them made me feel ashamed. But standing up on that stage that day gave me a hint of who I could be for them now. It was perhaps a good thing my parents weren't there, because I would have broken down crying myself.

This was really one of the biggest days in my life. Everything felt different. When I got home and lay on my bed, the room felt like it was spinning. I felt alive and powerful and free and I didn't want it to end. I wanted to be fluent and I felt that with work and technique I could be. That was the dangerous trap.

The Polo 98-D-1333

7

Faking it on national TV and in Honduras

I was on fire and on cloud nine and every other expression to express joy and it was the purest joy I have ever felt. I was free and powerful and supported. In the first week, I joined Toastmasters, an international speaking group. Liam, the family friend who'd given me a copy of the newspaper article, had been so inspired by me phoning and talking to him that he insisted I join up. Training in this way felt like an extension of my growing fluency and I embraced it. I stayed with the group for over a year and completed the basic speech training. Also in those first seven days, I phoned a dermatologist and went on acne medication. The treatment was drastic and involved monthly blood tests, but it promised to clear up my skin.

By the second week, I was looking for a new car. 88-MO-2911 had been a trusty steed but I wanted something newer and faster. My budget for a car was limited to €5,000, which was the amount I figured I could get for the Golf along with my savings. A real Mk2 Golf GTI would cost too much to run and service, and a newer Mk4 was too expensive. That left me with one option: go down a class and upgrade engine size while staying within the VW family. I was a huge fan of the Mk3 Polo which was, for a supermini, a grown-up car. The styling of the small hatchback was elegant, although a little conservative. Mk3 Polos reminded me of the original Golf from the 1970s and were comparable in size as well.

Car hunting was a real test for me. I was spending money, a lot of money from my impoverished perspective, and although it was a great contact experience I was intimidated because I knew I would be dealing with men. Dean came with me to various viewings and after a few disappointing weeks, I saw an ad for a 1.4 16-valve model in black, with alloy wheels, electric windows and power steering. The 16 valves made it a performance unit with a double overhead camshaft that produced around 100bhp, twice the power of any other car I had ever owned. I was excited.

We parked outside the address we'd been given, and a few minutes later 98-D-1333 came skidding around the corner into the driveway. That should have been the first red flag. The second should have been the boy racer who clambered out the car. The final flag should have been the modified GTI that sped into the drive after the Polo, from which a slightly older boy racer clambered out of. I ignored all three: this Polo was everything I was looking for.

I was slightly intimidated by the pair of boy racers, but I asked the obvious questions—service history, reason for sale and so on. Their answers were polite if a little vague; worse still they could tell I was eager to buy.

On my second viewing, I brought a mechanic and I noticed a few small dents I had missed before. The sinking feeling in my gut was an automotive spider sense and it was tingling. I should have walked away there and then, or at least tried to haggle down the price because of the service the car would require, but I didn't. I was too embarrassed to walk away and lose face or (and this is ridiculous) to let boy racer down by not taking the car off his hands in case he couldn't sell it. There is no doubt that I had come a long way in a short time but I hadn't yet learned to believe in myself or to know that I had every right to walk away if I chose. Taking this car off boy racer's hands wasn't my responsibility, yet I did so anyway. Handing over the cheque, the car was mine and driving home I prayed I hadn't made a huge mistake.

I drove 98-D-1333 home and parked it beside our house. Dad walked outside and asked, "Are you happy with it, Robert?"

Naturally, I lied. "Yes."

My acting skills weren't as honed as they are now and I suspect he saw through my feigned certainty. Dad was and is always the protector. He would do anything to keep his children safe, but in doing so one of them (me) hadn't learned to stand independently. Mum, who was always the first one to push us and let us fail, was always there to pick up the pieces. Mum congratulated me on my purchase but more for the fact that I had done it myself than for the car.

The fact that this car is still with me (well, sitting in the same hangar as the M3) shows that my initial fears were misplaced. It was around this time that the M3 was quietly put into storage in the newly built hangar down in Wexford. The hangar was a massive structure, built to store a helicopter with space for several more aircraft not to mention a few errant cars. Dad, being Dad, had the M3 neatly stored with a car cover and the battery on a trickle charge to keep it from going flat. And there the Beast would slumber. Everyone saw me making huge progress in my life and all assumed that I was well on my way to claiming the M3, so no big deal was made of its relocation. The value of these BMWs had begun to rise and the Beast was a Sport Evolution, the most sought-after model; storing it off road made financial as well as practical sense.

After changing cars, I had to get a job. I had been unemployed since leaving my career as a car cleaner. It was only February, but looking forward to the summer I decided to train as an ESL teacher. I finished a training course and was lucky enough to get a summer job with a school called English Language Studies Dublin (ELSD).

In May, I drove down to County Galway to attend my second

McGuire Programme course, a refresher for me and the opportunity to help other students as I had been helped. Seeing all the
familiar faces again was a thrill. A film crew from RTE, the Irish
National broadcaster Raidió Teilifís Éireann, was at the hotel in
Galway to make a documentary on the McGuire Programme,
following some of the new students on their four-day journey.
When I saw those cameras filming, I wanted to throw myself in
front of the lens. My skin was clearer now, not fully so but the
worst bad pustules had faded and I felt compelled to seek out the
limelight. I envied the people being recorded and wanted that to
be me. People on TV were special: they had courage and grace
and ability and other people admired them. Admiration and validation—that's want I wanted. To show the world that I was better;
to show all the bullies that they had failed and I had thrived. I was
fluent and my sexuality . . . well, that wasn't important. The film
crew's presence planted a seed in me, one that would take a few
years to grow but grow it did.

I went to most of my support meetings and four-day courses
on the McGuire Programme, training to become a primary coach
and a course instructor intern. I was working at English Language
Studies Dublin, initially as a summer camp teacher then becoming a permanent teacher at the school, where I meet my best
friend, Louise. Our boss called us dumb and dumber, which as
little too accurate for comfort. It was 2004, I was twenty-seven
and looking for another challenge when the opportunity to be on
television presented itself. Louise sent me a text message to say
that a daytime talk show was looking for a soap opera critic and
members of the public were invited to send audition videos to
apply for the position. I didn't watch soap operas and had abso-
lutely no knowledge of them, but when I called Louise she said I
should just send in a tape anyway. "What have you to lose?" she
said. Famous last words.

The Afternoon Show wanted a one-minute audition tape describing who I was and my passion for soap operas. I shot my tape quickly and ad-libbed most of it. My Toastmaster, McGuire and teaching experience were all paying off and a week later I received a phone call congratulating me: I had made the final cut of three potential critics. They would be sending a crew to my home to meet me and I had to brush up on soaps, fast. Louise though this was hilarious. The crew arrived at my home a few days later. They interviewed me and we spoke about my job, personal life and soap-watching habits.

I lied: I claimed I watched soaps after breaking up with my current girlfriend (Lie One); that I watched soaps on Sunday during the omnibus showings (Lie Two); and failed to mention that I was a recovering stutterer (Lie by Omission). I could have been honest and used the public platform to support the McGuire Programme, but I wanted to be fluent (and not at all gay either).

I walked into the RTE lobby and introduced myself to the girl at reception. An intern greeted me and led me to the Green Room, where I was to wait for *The Afternoon Show*'s researcher who would come to get me. There was food along with tea and coffee, so I grabbed a quick cup of tea and waited. Panic threatened, but I took a few breaths and focused on getting through the next few hours. *Just breathe and relax. You are here and you are good. Just keep it together.*

The researcher arrived and brought me up to a video room to view the footage that had been edited from the home visit. I thought it looked good. The show had me pitched as the "wild card" entry, but I was more likely to be the joker in this deck. An hour later I was standing behind the stage, ready for my cue. No one prepped me or told to look at Camera 2 or anything like that. Just focus on the presenter, they told me. The first few minutes on air went smoothly: a brief discussion about me during which they focused on my Toastmasters experience with no mention my stutter. The next part involved me reviewing a soap storyline I had been given and that was just like giving a prepared speech. We then took a break, the cameras stopped and the presenter offered to show me the answers to the soap opera pop quiz that was coming up next. I was mildly indignant—that would be cheating! I felt no fear, guilt or shame at this point in my performance. Back on air, I sat in the hot seat and the presenter proceeded to ask me rather simple soap questions. I got all of them wrong. After ten incorrect answers, she threw me a lifeline. "What is the name of the butcher on *Coronation Street*?"

"Fred," I shouted triumphantly. The presenter waited for his surname, which I didn't know, but she gave me the point anyway. My final score was one correct answer out of twenty. The production crew ushered me out of the hot seat and off the set. I was not offered the position of soap opera critic.

As I drove home texts filled the screen, mostly people congratulating me or calling me a mad thing. I never imagined little stuttering me would be in a real TV studio with lights and cameras and that it would feel fun and effortless. But my poor quiz results had exposed my lies, killing any credibility I had. Now I felt embarrassed, and when I returned home, I received two phone calls that only made me feel worse.

Dad was at the front door when I arrived, but I don't remember what we said to each other. I was in a suit and needed a shower and the first phone call came as I was drying off. It was Joe, the regional director of the McGuire Programme, a lovely man but slightly intimidating given his status and I was defensive when I rang him back.

I had always worked very hard on the programme and been a good recovering stutterer, followed all the rules and did what I was told. But I was tired of being known as "Robert the recovering stutterer" and there wasn't a "Robert the professional" or "Robert the lover."

"It was my choice not to disclose my stuttering nature," I told him. "I didn't do it to hurt you or the McGuire Programme; I did what I felt I needed to do regardless of whether it was right or wrong." To his credit, he congratulated me and we spoke for a few more minutes.

An hour and many cups of tea later, I received the second call, from a recent graduate of the programme. The funny thing about appearing on national television is that people do see you. Richard had just completed his first four-day course and he had my number because I was a primary coach. He was amazed at the fact that I had just been on television and asked if I had been scared and worried about my stutter. I arrogantly said that as an experienced graduate I could turn my technique on or off depending on the situation. After twenty minutes, I put the phone down and the knot in my gut told me I was a lying sack of shit. I couldn't turn my technique on or off at will—I had winged it through the whole thing. My arrogance would lead me astray again and again before I would come face-to-face with myself and be forced to accept my stutter. To make things worse I never spoke to that young man again, which I deeply regret.

I decided to continue pursuing a career in television regardless and I returned to college in 2006, just before my twenty-ninth birthday, when the Celtic tiger was at its height. These were optimistic times, and my institution of choice to study Television Presentation and Performance was Ballyfermot College of Further Education. This well-known media and arts college was one of the few public institutions to have practical media training courses as it had a purpose-built television studio. My course was a two-year diploma course that should have been condensed into one.

To support myself, I taught in the evenings at a city-centre EFL school while still attending my stuttering support meetings. The first year went by slowly. I fell into a groove of going to school and then work and being slightly amused by the media projects we were given, practical tasks like photography or Photoshop assignments that were light years away from the formal, highly analytical work I had written in Trinity College. Summer was approaching and I had fantasies of playing Resident Evil 4 on my Nintendo GameCube for the next few months. I thought I deserved the break but Mum had other ideas.

"Okay, Rob. So I think you should go away for the summer or else you can move out." Mum denies saying that, but I swear that is how I heard it. This as an ultimatum—how dare she!

In retaliation, I went online and googled "working holiday," deliberately picking the most dangerous and isolated place I could find. This turned out to be Honduras, and I would be there for two months, July and August. I told Mum what I had booked with glee. I was scared to death, though: Honduras and especially its capital city Tegucigalpa are not exactly five-star destinations, and getting there was my first solo journey on an airplane. The flight into Tegus, as the locals call it, was long and bumpy. There were a number of volunteers on the plane and we were collected by our agent after passing border control, which was essentially a shack just off the runway. We were all bundled into a VW camper van and sped away to our destination, a village building project three hours from the airport. There were about seven other young people on the bus all heading for the same place and they all saw this as a total adventure. They were younger and worldlier than I, with a thirst for life I seemed to lack; where I saw danger, disease and possible decapitation by machete, they saw fun and excitement.

After arriving at our village, I was greeted by my host mother. I called her Mama Anna and that was the extent to our communication. There was a British girl, Amanda, also staying in the house and we both had our own rooms with working lamps. The poverty on display was difficult to live with. Children with no clothes, wild dogs and chickens everywhere and one haggard, wizened old woman sitting at the entrance of her home. I had no Spanish and the volunteers who did acted as translators for the group. I just wanted to start doing something, anything to get me away from this scene and to alleviate my guilt at being a privileged white man. I picked up a machete and began hacking at the timber we had to strip. This was the work we did every day for weeks on end and, as we progressed, some volunteers began hooking up with each other for summer romances. I hated these people even more. They were comfortable in their own skins, kissing, laughing, loving, while I was still a very awkward mystery to myself and my own body.

Every few weeks, a new batch of volunteers would arrive for our project, in our village, deposited like terrified souls in the centre of the village where we would greet them. On one such drop-off was a cute blond American jock: sexy and muscular but with an attractive vulnerability and boy-next-door look.

The female volunteers found him instantly appealing and they collectively hurled themselves at his bags. One eager young woman even tried to claw the backpack off his back. The guys stood back, unimpressed, but I felt a little flutter in my chest.

Oh, crap.

Those fuzzy-wuzzy feelings again. Not wanting to explore them any further right there in public, I gave my attention to the welcome dinner we had arranged in the local restaurant. Food was a distraction, but only for a while. The weekend after Noah the American Jock arrived, we all went on a camping excursion to a lake site with a hotel and cabins about two hours out of the village.

This was my last weekend trip and it was like being at a five-star resort. The cabins had running hot water and light, a relief as the village we had been living in with our host families had only cold running water that didn't run consistently.

The twenty-three men and women had separate cabins but there weren't enough beds to go around and some of us were going to have to share double beds. On our first night at the resort, we all had beer and played pool, another rare treat. One of the older members of the group, a middle-aged man called Chris, began to assign the beds for all the men. As I stood in the bar listening to the arrangements, I remember thinking it would be exciting to share a bed with Noah. No sooner had I mentally chastised myself for that errant thought when the group decided that Noah and I would indeed be sharing a bed! A rush of adrenaline and my mind began to race; I wanted to speak up and say something but I didn't want to make a scene. Yet deep down, I was excited. This would be the closest I had ever been to being with a man in bed.

I decided to stop drinking immediately while everyone else proceeded to get wasted. When it came time to turn in for the night, the guys in my cabin fell into bed, including my new bed buddy. Noah took off his clothes, revealing a ripped, six-pack-touting body, and jumped into bed. I undressed displaying my less impressive skinny frame then slowly, cautiously pulled the sheet off the bed and lay as close to the edge of the mattress as was possible without actually falling out.

I lay there totally rigid and within minutes Noah was out for the count along with everyone else in the cabin. I could hear snoring from the other beds, and then Noah began to toss and turn in his sleep, letting out a groan. This made me rigid in a whole other way. I could feel the sweat begin to form on my back and forehead. God knows what he was dreaming about but I was having pretty vivid fantasies of my own. I could feel the heat of his body just beside me and he smelled amazing as well. The proximity to him was intoxicating. I didn't want to move in case he rolled over and I was too scared to do anything other than to lie there in a very aroused state. But, after an hour, I began to feel pain below the sheets; as aroused as I was, I couldn't stay that way all night. Several times I crept out of bed trying to relieve myself, assuming my erection would fade, but to no avail. Thoughts of blood clots or permanent organ damage began to race through my mind: *If I do get a blood clot and die will I still have an erection? Will my family be told that little detail?*

At about five o'clock in the morning the pain was becoming too much. I got out of the bed for what must have been the fifth time that night. I got dressed quietly and with difficulty (for the obvious reason), before creeping outside.

It was still dark and humid as I felt my way down toward the lake. Sitting on the grass by the shore, my erection gradually faded, but this brought no relief. Beneath the beauty of the Honduran sunrise, I sobbed silently. I was gay. My mind may not have been ready to accept that but my body sure was. I was in denial about my stutter and now, as I sat there with a fading erection, I decided that I could also avoid being gay by just never acting on those feelings. I would have to work hard to become someone who can make themselves feel things or rather, not feel things. Maybe acting was my answer?

8

Unleashing the Beast

If the first year of the television presentation course had dragged, the second was torture. We had a makeup class along with a cabaret end-of-term show, nothing to do with real television presentation skills. I felt we were dancing monkeys in a college that didn't take us seriously, but I wanted to finish and have something tangible to show for my twenty-four months of training. My frustration meant that I wasn't the most committed or gracious student to teach during the second year, I'm ashamed to say.

The idea of acting stuck with me, though; it would be more liberating, and the emotional work would be something I could use to keep my homosexuality in check. I began taking weekend acting classes that included an introduction to the Meisner technique, developed by the American actor and teacher Sanford Meisner. It is all about being present and living in the moment of a scene, following your gut instincts while servicing the script. Rather than reading from a teleprompter or scripts, it involved a lot of improvisation, which was fun.

I was on the cusp of turning thirty, and Dad decided this was a crucial transitional point in my life: it was time to take the Beast out of the hangar. Insurance was no longer an issue, and he claimed it was taking up valuable storage space even though he had sold the helicopter at this point. The timing was fortuitous as the Irish economy was about to implode with the collapse of the construction industry and the banking crisis that would lead to a global recession. In contrast, the E30 M3s in general and the Sport Evolution in particular had made the transition from old cars to desirable classics that were appreciating in value each day. If I didn't comply and drive the damn car, Dad might sell it. Like Mum forcing me to Honduras, now Dad was forcing me into the M3! Being forced into the driving seat of a black, highly conspicuous and thinly disguised track car that was probably worth more at a standstill than in my hands was not something I wanted to do. Getting the car roadworthy involved it being loaded onto a trailer and hauled to a BMW specialist in Naas, a county town in Kildare, nineteen miles west of Dublin. Driving along the N7 motorway, we noticed the attention the M3 was attracting, with people taking photos on their cell phones as we passed. The embarrassment I'd felt at school came flooding back to me. Dad always likes to stand out from the crowd (he'll deny that) but I was feeling very uncomfortable. Why not just leave the damn car in storage? There was all this other stuff going on in my life and I really didn't want to deal with one more challenge.

The specialists serviced the Beast and gave it a clean bill of health. After tax and insurance were arranged, the M3 sat in the driveway for a whole day, taunting me to take it out on the open road. I had never driven it alone and the experience was what I imagined having sex was like for the first time. Getting to learn the feel of a car is a private act, like getting to know the rhythms of a lover's body. Their scent, their touch and the responses. As I sat in the M3, I took a moment to feel the embrace of the seat and to enjoy the car's unique smell. I had done a lot of research on the M3 while it was being serviced and had read about the obvious difficulties like the left-hand driving position and the awkward dog-leg gearbox. The M3's S14 engine rattled into life as I turned the key. I could feel the vibrations through the pedals and gear stick as the whole car shook.

I decided to drive the familiar route to my cousin Dean's house. The Beast fidgeted endlessly and the clutch and gearbox conspired to groan and crunch at every traffic light. It felt tight and uncomfortable and I was tired and sore. *If this is truly what intercourse is like, then sod it, I can do without.* By the time I arrived at Dean's, my back was drenched in sweat, my foot and wrist ached and I was disappointed in the car with no urge to have another drive in it. Now, like sex, there is an element of practice and, I will admit, I could have tickled the accelerator a little more, been more gentle with the gear stick and tried to listen to the messages the car was sending me back. I decided I wasn't ready to give up on it yet. If the automotive world hailed this car as driving nirvana, they surely couldn't be wrong. The problem turned out to be me, the driver, and not the car. I was to discover that the Beast really isn't a delicate machine and I was being too gentle. A road trip to Tullamore to work on an acting scene with a friend was the day I would really fall in love with this car.

Tullamore was a ninety-minute drive west of Dublin along the M4 and M6 motorways and then on to the narrower, more twisty traditional back roads. Our journey began in Dublin with a fuel stop and I was still uncomfortable with the attention this car garnered; men would stop and ask me about the car and if it was for sale and I had no idea how to react without stuttering or, worse, blushing. I felt like a fake as it wasn't even really my car. Halfway through the journey, I came to a motorway toll-booth and the M3's left-hand drive configuration meant I had to get out of the car, walk around to the booth and pay. More inconvenience and embarrassment—I was getting angry. The anger was directed at the Beast and I began to manhandle it. No more gentle inputs. I stabbed the clutch and floored the accelerator. The M3 screamed down the road. I pushed each gear past 4,500 rpm and turned off the motorway onto the back roads. Something amazing was happening. The car began to come alive. Gone was the fidgeting, as the suspension began to find its rhythm, and we swept through the bends. The engine at higher revs was singing with a razor-sharp response I had never felt before. I could feel the chassis underfoot, dancing. It felt fluid and transparent and the steering was writhing in my hands.

I felt alive in a way I hadn't felt for years. The anger I'd been sitting on all my life was unleashed on the car; in any other situation, I would have regained control and stifled my anger because it frightened me. I was so mad all the time at everything and everyone, but this car came alive because of it. It needed that push and I needed the freedom to push. I spent all my life being meek, accommodating and apologetic to every bloody eejit out there. I had no idea what I was capable of and right now I was been shown by the Beast. I wasn't afraid of crashing and I wasn't afraid that we were speeding, because the M3 didn't need high speeds to dance, it needed a committed driver—me. I felt my own body working in unison with the car. The inputs had to be assertive and I was excited. I was laughing with joy. Here I was living in the moment, trusting myself and the car to do what we both knew to do and I discovered what the car's legacy was in that instant: true freedom. Freedom from all the burdens I had placed on myself. I felt like a child once more and it was one of the best days of my life. By connecting with the car, I had connected with a dead part of myself, a part I thought would never come alive.

Over the next few days and weeks that feeling faded. I wanted to feel that connection all the time, without having to go for a vigorous drive every day. The idea of acting stuck with me. The performance aspect stroked my ego and the skill set of emotional authenticity and imagination felt to me like the way to go to learn how to access and deal with myself in a healthy way. I had been in acting school in Dublin on a part-time basis now for a number of years and was still teaching ESL. It was 2009, I was in my early thirties and I felt time was running out. Susan had moved to San Diego the year before for graduate school and Jenny was in a serious long-term relationship with her boyfriend Paudie (short for Padraig in Gaelic, Patrick in English). I decided to go to acting school in Vancouver, Canada, because that was where *Stargate SG-1* and *Atlantis* were made along with *Battlestar Galactica*, shows that had filled the void left when *Star Trek* had gone off the air. In many ways, *Stargate* had been a sleeper; the initial few seasons were rough but, as the show found its feet, it got better and better. It was pure comfort television and as I learned more about acting, and acting in a sci-fi show with all the special effects, my respect for these actors grew. I didn't want to be a stage actor, I wanted to be a sci-fi actor, sitting on the bridge of a battlecruiser spooling up the hyperdrive as aliens attacked. I would get to phone home and brag to all the people in Dublin that I had saved Earth, again. I also had a bit of a crush on Amanda Tapping's character Samantha Carter, but not in a sexual way. She had evolved from a naïve scientist on *SG-1* to the leader of the Atlantis expedition on the spin-off show, *Atlantis*. She was beautiful and clever but had terrible luck with men. Some part of me fancied myself to be like her in that way. Maybe if I became a successful actor in Vancouver, I would attract the man of my dreams and be happy. Gay marriage was legal in Canada too, so that was another incentive to pack my bags. The biggest issue was money. ESL did not pay well but I had managed to save a moderate amount of money by living at home. If this crazy notion was to become a reality, it would mean sacrificing something much closer to my heart and it was now sitting parked outside in the driveway.

Mum was in the kitchen the day I plucked up enough courage to say, "I want to go to acting school in Vancouver. But it may mean selling the M3."

Mum's reaction was unexpected. She didn't seem surprised and just said, "You will have to talk to your father."

If I had her on my side, Dad would follow suit and I know in my heart Mum wanted me to get away from home. I suspect she knew I was gay and that I needed space to explore it. Acting and going to Vancouver was merely a way to do this. To my shock, Dad didn't seem too bothered by the idea of me going to acting school and selling the M3. But that would mean splitting the proceeds among Jenny, Susan and myself and, being self-serving, I wanted to keep the car in storage and take out a loan against the Beast, which was still appreciating in value. I could always sell it later if I returned from Vancouver.

It was agreed that I should talk to the bank and see what kind of loan I would qualify for, so the next day (Monday), I phoned and arranged a meeting with the loan officer for the following Thursday. I did my research on the current value of the M3 to act as collateral towards a loan: it was worth around £55,000. I washed and waxed the Beast in case the loan officer wanted to inspect the car. Thursday came and there we were, 90-D-41990 and I in the bank car park like a knight and his warhorse. For ten minutes, I sat in the Beast fiddling with my file of facts and trying to breathe to get some stuttering technique going. Stuttering would make me look weak and nervous, as if I was trying to scam this guy, which I suppose I was. What kind of actor stutters? The meeting lasted all of five minutes; I think I lost the battle when the loan officer asked me why I wanted the money.

"I want to go to Vancouver and be a sci-fi actor with Amanda Tapping and go through the Stargate to save Earth," I bleated out enthusiastically. He looked at me dumbfounded. I tried to show him my M3 facts and figures but he ran me out of the office quicker than the Borg can say "Resistance is futile." No loan for me.

I'd found an acting school in downtown Vancouver that offered a six-month training programme and I could cover the cost with my life savings. Living expenses as a student at that time were another matter, yet something inside screamed: take the chance! It looked like the only option was to sell the M3. Arriving home and walking into the kitchen, I went for the kettle. If I was going to have my car ripped away from me in my final attempt to carve out some kind of existence, I was going to do it with a cup of tea in my hand. Mum walked into the kitchen. She knew it hadn't gone well by my silent skulk into the house.

"Well, how did it go?"

"Not well," I said. "Officially, I am not a student anymore so I do not qualify for a student loan and I am not earning enough to qualify for any other kind of loan." It all sounded very reasonable.

"Do you really want to do this?" Mum asked

"Yes."

"Why?"

"Because I need to do this now before I really am too old."

It was the truth. I could keep the M3 and live at home forever, but I wanted to be like Susan. I wanted to be away, discovering myself, living away from people who knew me. I had allowed myself to be defined by others all my life and I really did want to be an actor. I wanted to travel and even if I failed, like with the bank earlier, I wanted to know on my death bed that, at the very least, I had tried.

"Okay. You pay for the school with your savings. I will find the extra money you need, and you can pay me back. Call the acting school and book your flights," Mum said.

Together we worked out a deal: Mum would give me the balance of money I needed to top up what I had saved and if, when it came time to repay her, I couldn't, then I would sell the M3. I will love her until the end of time for that act of kindness. Within a week, I was enrolled in the Vancouver Acting School (VAS) and had found a host family to live with for my first months there. Both the M3 and my own car, 98-D-1333, went into storage in the hangar and I had my bags packed, ready to fly off and begin a new chapter in my life, secure in the knowledge that the Beast was safe.

9

Hot men and "Funeral Blues"

Some poor soul at Air Canada was probably tasked with repairing the claw marks found on Seat 27B. I have to take responsibility for that. There wasn't a relaxed moment on the twelve-hour flight to Vancouver. Going through immigration for the first time was nerve-wracking. When the border control guard asked where I was from and what I was studying, my response was the same the one I'd given the bank loan officer; it sounded no less crazy the second time. I had opted to stay with a host family because I hoped they would be maple-syrup-eating, hockey-obsessed Canadians who would help me settle into the city. Instead, they were a lovely Filipino family who had no idea what I was doing in Vancouver and thankfully gave me a wide berth for the month I lived with them before moving into another rented room with an anti-social roommate.

I opened a bank account and bought a laptop and cell phone within twenty-four hours. I had a lifeline to home and a way to communicate with my acting school. We had a brief introduction session on the Friday before classes started. I discovered I was one of around forty students there, which included an eclectic mix of mostly Canadians, a few Americans, two people from the UK, plus myself and an Irish girl from Cork.

The weekend came and went and Monday was the official beginning of my actor training in Vancouver. We were divided into two groups of twenty students each, with the groups to be changed every month so that we would get an opportunity to work with as many people as possible over the six-month semester. The curriculum was divided into scene study, improvisation, movement, camera technique and voice work. Nothing I hadn't done at home but now the stakes were higher. My accent was something I worked hard on, but with the stutter and increased stress, I found it all very challenging.

Movement class was a little better but I preferred improvisation, as we had no scripts to read from. Still, I couldn't help but wonder if I wasn't making a huge mistake. My first breakthrough occurred in scene study class with the emotionally powerful and beautiful teacher, Amber. Our first assignment was to perform a scene to camera. Mine was the funeral monologue from *Four Weddings and a Funeral*. In the 1994 film, John Hannah brilliantly portrayed a man grieving after the death of his partner. The character's eulogy for his deceased lover Gareth is passionate and beautiful, and concludes with W.H. Auden's "Funeral Blues." This man was his life, his love, his everything. The fact that it was a "he" was one of my problems but the actor in me realized that whether it was a man or woman, it really didn't matter. What did matter was finding those emotions.

Truthfully, I had never loved like that in my life. Sure, I loved my family but to really love someone, that was alien. I could try to fake it but I was passed that stage. I wanted to be a good actor and some part of me wanted to feel what love was like. I tried to imagine people I was close to—my parents, my sisters—but that felt wrong. I tried to fantasize about my dream woman and, unsurprisingly, nothing much happened. The only emotional attachment that felt genuine was my love for the Beast but would that be enough? I doubted it. I had to go somewhere I really didn't want to go. I remembered the feelings I'd felt for Alan and Keith and the other hot men I had encountered over the years and began to imagine a man. It felt wrong. I felt dirty when I imagined hairy arms and chests that stirred another part of my body. I told myself that this was okay, that it was part of my training and that it was only acting after all.

Gradually, I allowed myself the freedom to imagine a real boy-friend and this is where I began to run into difficulty. I'd never imagined myself on a date with a man, or holding hands, or just doing simple relationship things. That would have made my homo-sexuality too real. Nothing felt real and I needed something more concrete. After hours searching the net for inspiration, I settled on a certain famous Silver Fox reporter. He was professional, brave and rather adorable and he became the model for my dead lover, Gareth. I printed out a few pictures of him and began to create our life together. How did we meet? What was our first date?

Did he snore? These aspects of acting I loved. The pure crea-tion of it all. I could make this man my perfect partner. I had a few weeks to prepare the scene and pick a costume. Each week in Amber's class the scene changed and evolved. I loved having this little secret from my classmates. Gradually, it no longer felt dirty or wrong to imagine myself with a man. I didn't think I deserved someone like my Gareth. Why would he date me? I was fretting about my imaginary boyfriend and him leaving me. At home in my room, I could just be with these bizarre feelings.

Over the three-week preparation period, I imagined various scenarios with Gareth. I imagined myself in the M3, driving to pick him up. Gareth would buy me flowers that would be put in the boot (not on the back seats as pollen can stain the cloth) and our date would begin with a walk on the beach with some Xbox gaming by candlelight later. Nothing like saving Earth together to strengthen the bonds between people. Childish as this fantasy was, it was groundbreaking for me: I was coming out to myself for the first time. In the fantasy, I began to feel something like actual love towards a man, and now it began to feel right.

These recorded monologues were to be the first material to be graded, so the pressure was on us all. I was given one rough take and only began to feel emotional towards the end of the monologue. The poem, although beautiful, was causing me trouble as the words were so flowery and alien. I was angry that it wasn't working—I was skating over the emotions, not really letting myself feel them. The contradiction was that I needed to be perfect, to perform the scene cleanly and precisely, but if I let myself get emotional, it could be messy and not what I wanted at all.

Amber told me to start the scene again immediately after finishing. This time my anger was about my loneliness and pain. As I spoke the words of the monologue, those imagined scenes with Gareth melted away, but the raw feelings remained. The tears now flowing down my cheeks weren't for a fake boyfriend or for the M3. They were for me. The scene is about the grief for a life lost. For me it was for a life not lived, a life missed, a life denied. I wanted to stand proud and talk about a real boyfriend. I was beginning to accept my sexuality.

The next step came at the Christmas party, days before I was due to fly home for a two-week vacation. In between all the dancing and screaming, I snuck outside the building. Having begun to accept myself as gay, I felt a kind of surrender to the whole situation. When I got outside the school building, I saw one of my classmates alone on the step. I sat down beside Cat, and we both just stared quietly at the ground.

"Too much excitement?" I asked her.

"Yeah, I just needed some air" she replied.

"I know. Me too. It's been a crazy few months, hey?"

We sat there in silence for a few minutes. Normally that kind of silence would freak me out, but it felt right in that moment.

"I think I'm bisexual," Cat said.

"I think I'm gay," I replied. I had never told anyone that before and I felt free in giving it life. We didn't need words. We sat there for a few more minutes and then hugged and went back to the party. It was the most intimate moment of my life so far.

My trip home was a strange one. I was not ready to say what was going on with me. When asked about acting school, my stutter would suddenly flare up. I avoided words and names and said I was just overwhelmed to be home. But it was all too brief a break. Back in Vancouver, the pressure at VAS ramped up dramatically. Talk of agents, headshots and end-of-term showcases flowed around with enthusiasm. It didn't mean that much to me as I was preoccupied with my own personal exploration. Two specific classes finally broke me out of the closet.

The first was an emotion dance exercise. In theory, it should have been fun but I hated dancing. We had to pick songs the elicited different emotions in us and, being a total nerd, the happy song I picked was *Walking on Sunshine* by Katrina and the Waves. It was a song used to advertise the Amiga 500 Plus (Dean and Leon's computer) twenty years earlier. The sad song was *Hippipolla* by Sigur Ros and my rock song was Dan Bush's *Dare* from *The Transformers: The Movie*. I was embarrassed by my selections, as I didn't really have a strong passion for music and wondered what people thought of my taste. I hoped they didn't think it was too gay. When my turn came, I tried. I really, really tried. I wanted to be an actor and I decided to let myself go.

"You have to feel the music," Amber instructed. "This isn't a learning exercise. Trust your body and instincts."

So I did. I looked like a child swinging his arms, but it was truly me and broke the last crack in my defences before the floodgates opened.

A few weeks later, Amber hit our class with another emotionally themed exercise involving visualization. I was still reeling from the dance exercise and was happy that this exercise started off seemingly innocuous enough. Each student was tasked with sitting in a chair placed in front of the class with Amber in the corner of the room giving verbal instructions and guidance through the visualization exercise. Like the dance exercise before it, it was designed to help us actors-in training use our imaginations to visualize scenarios. This was vital for all the green-screen and CGI effects that are used in modern shows and movies. I went on the second day, and I was pretty calm about it.

Watching others go before me was a fascinating experience as we sat and listened to their visual journey and tried to imagine it as best we could ourselves. When my turn came, I sat on the chair at the top of the room and shut my eyes. I was breathing using my costal diaphragm as this was part of the exercise to help us relax and visualize.

"Where are you?" Amber asked. My mind went home to Grafton Street. I saw myself beside the St. Stephen's Green Shopping Centre; it was a sunny day and there were people all around me. I described this scene to the class being as detailed as I could be, even down to the pigeons flying around. This was home and I felt so happy to be there.

"Start walking down the street and describe what you see," Amber said. I did and was able to describe the spot where I had given my McGuire Programme soapbox speech, the Burger King and Bank of Ireland on the right-hand side of the road. There was a River Island on the left-hand side and, as I reached the end of the street, I saw the Molly Malone statue standing proudly on the corner. Trinity College's main entrance was just around Grafton Street flowing onto College Green. This all felt so vivid and real.

"Look around the road," Amber said. "What do you see?"

Now, for whatever reason, I saw a white Porsche parked on the side of the road, specifically a Porsche 911 GT2.

"How do you feel?" she asked

"I'm happy. I feel safe." I said, my eyes still shut. *Why is that? Expensive cars make me nervous. I'll never enough money to own one.* A few seconds of silence.

"Keep looking around Rob, and keep moving," said Amber. "Describe what you see."

I looked to my right, down Nassau Street. I saw Trinity College's back entrance at the junction between Nassau and Dawson Street, which runs parallel to Grafton Street. It's the entrance I had used frequently during my five years there.

"Tell us more, give us as much detail as you can." Amber's voice encouraged me.

The gate I was imagining in my mind was ornate. Wait. This isn't right, it's the front gate that is ornate, not the Dawson Street one. I was beginning to get confused and annoyed, not sure if I was remembering or just making it up as I went. My time at college was not my happiest, so why was I there at Trinity in this exercise?

Amber sensed my anxiety. "Stay calm and let your imagination flow."

In my mind, I walked towards the entrance and saw a figure walking out towards me. My heart began to beat faster. Why was I imagining this? I wanted to stop the exercise because it was taking on a life of its own, but a part of me needed to go on. A man was walking towards me. It was Keith, the handsome ginger project leader. I felt a bead of sweat roll down my back as I sat tensely on the chair.

"Who do you see? Tell us about him," Amber urged me.

I began to say, "An old friend," but stopped. I wanted to say, "Someone I'm attracted to." My heart was thumping in my chest and, although I knew I was in class far away, in that moment I was in Dublin, looking at Keith face-to-face. I wasn't scared or embarrassed. I was excited and then nervous. This figure in front of me felt like my innate sexuality making itself manifest. Keith walked towards me and hugged me. I could feel the warmth of his body and the closeness of his embrace. It felt like home—safe and peaceful. I began to cry. This is what I had been running from my whole life. Not Keith per se but what he represented: my heart's desire, and I was holding on to him for dear life, not wanting to let go or for the fantasy to end.

Amber ended the exercise and, as I returned to myself and the room, I felt exposed and in danger. Then I began to get angry.

"What are you thinking?" Amber asked.

"I've wasted so much time and for what?" I sobbed.

"You can leave the room, Robert," Amber said.

I did. I left the school and found myself on a bench looking out onto North Vancouver. My sexuality was out of the bag and life wouldn't ever be the same again. I returned to school to try to explain my behaviour but Amber had already left.

There was another teacher there, a cool lesbian teacher called Lily. She owned her sexuality so completely that I had deliberately avoided getting too close to her. I found it both ironic and comforting that she was the one I was now reaching out to. I asked to speak to her outside and, when we were in the hall, all I could say to her was, "I'm gay."

What she gave me then was what I needed most: a hug. Simple human contact and comfort from someone who understood what I was going through. Lily must have said something to me but I don't remember what. I would like to think it was something like "I am so proud of you" or "You will be okay." I wanted to ask her so many questions but, in the moment, words escaped me. However, I am so grateful to her for being there for me.

With all this going on, I'd be lying if I claimed I was totally focused on my actor training. We were now in March, our final month, and I had had my headshots taken and had been successful in getting into the showcase at the end of the semester with my scene partner Brianna. We were doing a scene from the movie Happiness, about a man discovering himself and reclaiming his power—life imitating art. My stutter at this point was pretty much out of control and I found myself really struggling with the scene. It worked for this character but I felt ineffective and deflated. What the hell was I doing in acting school? I assumed my speech was all over the place because I was coming out and emotionally stressed. The whole time in Vancouver, living alone and dealing with life, was also new and stressful. But I needed my speech to be more manageable if I was ever going to be an effective working actor. The other massive issue was my legal status. I wasn't permitted to work in Canada and I knew I was going home at the end of the month. Did I feel ready or complete? No, but I was out of money. In a desperate effort to stay, I applied online for a one-year working holiday visa through the youth travel agency USIT in Dublin about a week before I flew home. I was number 996 on the waiting list and so I had to make peace with the idea that I was leaving Vancouver for good.

On my last night in the city, the whole class went out to celebrate our graduation. I even had two beers and made the decision to start telling people I was gay. If they turned out to be raging homophobes, I'd be gone the next day. Telling people was like starting a cold car engine. I stuttered through my initial attempt to my close friends, Sachi and Sophie. They were thrilled and not surprised. Then I told Vivian, who laughed and commented rather vulgarly that a hole was a hole, eh? I cringed. It was too soon for me to really know what to say to that.

As the night went on, I got into my stride and it was very much like making my stuttering disclosures. No one was that surprised and I decided to celebrate my victory with another pint, which I shouldn't have.

10

If you all knew, why the hell didn't you tell me?

My flight home was on Thursday, March 18, 2010, the day after St. Patrick's Day and I was late to the airport and, coming out at thirty-two, really rather late to my own party too.

Running on adrenaline after packing the night before and sleeping for no more than four hours, I headed to the security checkpoint, my backpack slung over my shoulder. Everything will be fine as soon as you get home and come out, I told myself. What I should have told myself was, be careful what you put in your carry-on luggage. As my bag passed through the X-ray scanner, alarm bells began to ring in my head, followed by the literal kind. The officer pulled my backpack out of the scanner, opened it and using a pen extracted a pair of handcuffs, which he dangled like a pair of dirty underwear. People in the line behind me sniggered, presumably thinking I was some kind of kinky sex beast. I wish. As a still very much non-practising virgin, I was close to shouting out that fact to ease my embarrassment, but this was an airport and I just needed to get home and come out to my family before I lost my nerve. I explained to the officer that I was an actor and showed him one of my new fancy business cards printed just the day before.

The officer didn't look convinced, so I decided further elaboration was required. "Look, I'm gay and I'm flying home to come out to my family! Keep the cuffs—they were for a scene, which kind of sucked anyway because I wasn't exactly on top of my game . . . so, please, please, just let me get on the plane!"

He now looked dumbfounded and let me through the checkpoint but kept the cuffs. I arrived at the gate with only minutes to spare.

The flight from Vancouver to London was a blur. I tried to sleep but couldn't. I didn't fear telling my family I was gay; I knew I would be accepted or, at the very least, tolerated—but it would change things.

I decided to tell Mum and Dad together first, then go from there. Posting it on Facebook or only telling a few people wasn't for me. I had to do this steadily, face-to-face and own it; it was an important way to show respect for the people I felt deserved it. If I was going to come out, I going to do it big and completely. Never again would I hide my sexuality.

The stopover in London provided some relief in the form of the latest issue of BMW Car magazine, which had a feature on the new 5-series (F10). I tried to read but couldn't, and clung to the magazine like a safety blanket until the plane set down in Dublin. I was home. I can't remember why no one greeted me at the airport; I imagine I must have told them I would get a cab and make my own way home in case the flight was delayed. Dad gets snarky at the airport at the best of times, having to park and walk and do what the airport authorities tell him. I'm sure I wanted him and Mum as calm as possible for my coming-out announcement.

Passing up my traditional cup of tea in the airport lounge, I jumped into a cab and told the driver to take me home. My speech was already faltering at this point and I blocked on more than one occasion. Thankfully, I didn't need to say much as he talked incessantly about Irish politics and the like, while I tried to breathe and prepare myself for the admission ahead. When I eventually escaped his one-sided diatribe, I was looking at the gates of my house. I had walked through these gates for years but today I felt like a stranger and part of me wanted to run away.

Muscle memory allowed me to enter the code to open the gate. I walked slowly up the path, telling myself I could do this. It felt like a death, but this was the death of lies and hiding and the easier path, which was a good thing. Once I said those three little words there would be no going back.

As I got closer to the house I saw 98-D-1333 sitting in its usual space, freshly washed, and I could smell the faint scent of wax wafting from it. Dad had obviously taken it out of the hangar and cleaned it for me. I didn't have the keys but I stopped and reached out my hand to the car. The metal was cold to the touch but now I really felt like I was home.

Dad had threatened to change the locks, but like the gate code, my door key still worked. I heard them both in the kitchen. I had been travelling for around fourteen hours, including the connecting flight from London to Dublin. With the eight-hour time difference between Vancouver and Dublin, by now this was Friday and lunchtime. Dad greeted me at the door, dressed in his casual attire of tracksuit bottoms and horribly fitting white cotton T-shirt.

"Welcome home, son!" he said as he hugged me. "Did you notice the Polo out there? I had it cleaned yesterday." He took my bag and I went into the hall. I should have felt huge relief but my fear was suddenly escalating.

I went into the kitchen to find Mum there in her dressing gown and she hugged me too. "Welcome home! Was the flight okay?" I said it was fine and that I needed to take a quick shower.

"Good, I'm about to cook lunch. Do you want white and black pudding?" Mum asked.

"Just white," I responded as I ducked out to my room.

Being back in my own room brought no relief. It was bizarre. There was my single bed and desk and Xbox 360 and PlayStation 2 sitting just where I'd left them. This was my room and yet it felt like someone else's, including the awesome USS *Defiant* model from *Star Trek: Deep Space Nine* on my desk. They all felt like they belonged to someone else. Get into the shower. I was lucky to have an en suite in my bedroom, one of the very practical reasons for not moving out. The hot water had no effect on my tense muscles. Feeling my nerve slip, I was mad at myself for the weakness. Grabbing some clean clothes from my suitcase, I went back into the kitchen, which smelled deliciously of Mum's traditional Irish fry-up of bacon, sausage, baked beans and white pudding. I sat down at the table at my usual place and looked at the plate in front of me. I nearly began eating but didn't. Staring at my knees, unable to look either of them in the face, I mumbled, "I have to tell you something . . ."

Long dramatic pause.

". . . I'm gay."

Waiting for their response was the most terrifying moment.

I looked up. To my surprise, Dad was the one who was crying.

"Why didn't you tell us this sooner? All those years of struggling." I had no answer. But he got up and came over to me and we hugged. The relief was immense.

Mum sat with her arms across her chest. "I've known for years," she said. I couldn't read what was going on in her mind quite so easily. Mum claims to have no tear ducts, but I assumed she was just relieved more than anything else. She'd been the one who had supported my plan to go to Vancouver and agreed to keep the Beast in storage, and here I was finally admitting the truth to her. "Robert," she said, "the fact that you never brought a girl home made it rather obvious."

Jenny, who was still living in Dublin at the time, came up to the house for dinner. I sat her down in the kitchen alone and told her. She looked surprised, which shocked me a little. I assumed that, like my parents, she had suspected for years too.

"I am sorry I haven't been the big brother you or Susan deserve," I said. "I have spent years being jealous of how amazing you both are in my eyes. I am so sorry, Jenny, and I love you. You know that, right?" Jenny, like Mum, can be hard to read. But I meant what I said. I have always looked up to her as someone with real power and beauty. She is harder-edged than me and I knew this was something I would need to learn on this journey of coming out. We hugged and spoke for a while about my plans but I really wasn't thinking beyond the next day or two. I had made a list of people to come out too and that was my mission.

Susan was next on my list. I was more nervous about calling her and felt grateful that I had a screen and thousands of miles separating us. Susan had questioned my choice to go to Vancouver to pursue acting and was rather demanding in extracting an answer from me as to why I was doing it. As she was a psychologist-in-training, I felt obliged to have an answer to give her. Deep down I knew I was doing it to explore myself and, by extension, my sexuality, but I hadn't been ready to say that six months earlier. So after Jenny had gone home and I had unpacked, I fired up the computer and dialled Susan.

"How was the trip back?" she asked

"Fine," I said. "Listen, I have some news. I am gay." I got it out as rapidly as I could. Like Jenny, she looked surprised. I was slightly annoyed with her.

"I thought you had guessed that was why I was going to Vancouver," I said to her.

She took a second or two to consider my statement. "I suspected and hoped you would figure things out and I am happy the acting helped."

"Yeah, me too." She had no idea how much the acting helped.

"Well, there are lots of hot boys here in California. You should come and visit soon!"

JUST ONE MORE DRIVE

That's Susan—never one to miss a beat. We spoke for a little while longer and I let her go.

By the end of the night I was truly exhausted but content. My family had my back, and it didn't matter what anyone else thought. I felt lighter and more at peace than I could remember ever feeling. I was now taking real action and beginning to grow into the man I knew I could be.

On my second day being officially gay, I told Nana O'Brien. I had written to her while I was in Vancouver and I knew she was pretty okay with the gay thing, being a rather open-minded woman, yet I felt dishonest in a way. Dad's question of why I had suffered and waited so long to come out stuck in my head. I had grown very close to Nana O'Brien over the years and wondered if she would be angry that I hadn't confided in her. Either way, I was about to find out as I drove up the driveway to her house.

She welcomed me in and I made us both a cup of tea before sitting down. I wasn't sure how to phrase what I had to tell her. I didn't want to say, "I'm a homosexual," or "Hey, Nana, I like dudes."

So I began with, "I have some news . . ."

When I got the words out, she shocked me by jumping up and giving me a huge hug. The woman was in her early eighties but she moved quicker than I had ever seen her move. After releasing me from her fierce grip, she told me she had suspected that for years.

Apparently, Dad had come to her with his own suspicions about my sexuality and had asked her for advice. Nana, being an experienced mother and grandmother, correctly told him to wait and let me come to him. That piece of advice is one hundred percent correct and fundamental to coming out. Everyone may suspect, or know, but they aren't the ones who have to live with it; forcing someone out of the closet before they are ready is wrong and damaging. It felt great to tell her, given her age and what her generation was brought up to believe by the Catholic Church. Now my only problem is getting pressured to find a nice man every time I visit her.

After Nana O'Brien, I had to visit Nana Iremonger in the nursing home. Mum told her mother, but I still wanted to stop by and talk to her in person. As with Nana O'Brien, I was nervous. I would be the only gay grandchild on that side of the family and I was beginning to feel stupid about not coming out sooner. Nana Iremonger was a little older, in her early nineties, and I wanted to make sure she understood what gay in this context meant. "Gay" could also mean "happy" to some people, so I had to broach the subject carefully.

So there I was, sitting on her special motorized bed and the metal frame was digging into my side. Nana was perched in her chair with her newspaper and TV remote beside her. She wore large glasses that made her look rather owl-like. As Mum had already told her, I decided to just jump straight in.

I said, "So you know I like men? Yeah?"

She looked at me and just said, "That's great news, Robert!"

As we were in a nursing home with open doors, I wasn't going to overload the poor woman with details, but Mum reassured me that she did indeed understand and was very proud of me for coming out. I felt very lucky that my grandmothers still saw their grandson as a person, not just as a newly minted, confused and untested gay person.

My third day officially gay, I gathered my cousins Dean, Leon and Zara together at Leon's and his partner Jen's house. This disclosure should have been easy but I spent the first twenty minutes in the toilet working up the nerve to go down and tell them. I sat down on the couch beside Dean, with Zara and Leon on the opposite couch. Jen was making the tea.

I just said, "Listen, guys. I'm gay."

"Oh, okay," said Leon.

Then he shouted towards the kitchen, "Jen, Rob's gay."

Dean just said, "Cool."

Zara took the opportunity to ask a totally inappropriate question followed by a gross gesture. Again, no drama! I was indignant. If I had known it was going to be like this I might have come out years earlier. It was Zara's reaction that really meant a lot to me. I appreciated that Dean and Leon were fine with it but it was such an underwhelming reaction that I was unsure that they, like my Nana Iremonger, really didn't get the enormity of it for me. I had no bloody idea what being gay meant and Zara having fun with me about the sexual side signalled her approval and willingness to engage me with it. I hadn't had sex yet and I was petrified. I already felt weird and old and now rather stupid too. You had to either laugh or cry, and Zara had me in fits of laughter. There was an openness there that I really needed.

After that night my relationship with Zara grew and we became closer, talking about men in a filthy and hilarious manner. It was how I chose to do it because sex, and gay sex especially, can be such a loaded issue. But at its core, it should be no different to any other kind of sex. Either way, Zara gave me a gift that night. I love Jenny and Susan but have never felt the freedom to talk to them the way I do with Zara. It is not a bad thing, just different.

On Day Four I found myself outside my best friend Louise's door. We had formed a strong relationship over the years and we had seen each other through some very rough times. Like Zara, there was an irreverence to our relationship. We supported each other through everything, made a holy show of ourselves in public and most of all just laughed together.

After my appearance on television, Louise had developed the habit of shouting out the word "Fred" on random occasions that had us in stitches laughing. I knew she had my back and I knew I could be one hundred percent honest with her regarding my feelings, because under the joviality was an honesty that I value in our friendship more than anything else.

When I told her I was gay she reacted like everyone else. By now I was furious and blurted out, "Well if everyone knew, why the fuck did no one ever say anything! I'm exhausted going around coming out like some kind of travelling circus attraction!"

She looked at me and took my hand. "Rob, no one could say anything. You had to come to terms with it yourself—that was what was important, not whether we knew or not. I'm proud of you."

Knowing she was right still didn't make it easier to hear. This wasn't about others; it was about me. My ego was getting in the way—I was the one responsible for my own suffering and that was a bitter pill to swallow.

I would continue to come out to other family, friends and even McGuire graduates as well but the people I had talked to over the last few days were the most important and it motivated me to keep moving. I had years to make up for and as emotionally exhausted as I was, I felt excited for what was to come next and it turned out to be beer and sex.

11

Men, mothers and bedsheets

So far, everyone was fine, if not more excited, with me being gay. The fear I had felt about coming out gave way to uncertainty and anxiety. I was thirty-two years old, clueless and, worst of all, impatient; baby steps were not the way to catch up on all I had missed, and so I went in search of support and guidance from the only gay man I knew.

I had met Matthew in one of the first acting classes I'd taken and we had kept in touch sporadically over the years. Always unspoken and unacknowledged in our acquaintance was the fact that I was a closeted gay, so now I felt the need to tell him I was finally out. I was legitimately looking for advice from him and, if more were to happen in a physical sense, I wasn't going to run away. I needed to prove to myself that I was gay and there was really only one way to do that. Poor Matthew should have known better and followed the first rule of dealing with a newly-out hot mess: handle with extreme care and don't provide him with copious amounts of beer, which will naturally ease inhibitions.

We arranged to meet, and I told Mum I was going out to meet a friend. I had never mentioned Matthew by name to her before but she somehow knew who he was.

"Be careful," she said with a slightly suspicious tone. I suspect she knew where this was all going before I did. Her powers of perception troubled me but I was too distracted about my midday meeting with Matthew to give them much thought.

I met him in the beer garden of a bar in the centre of Dublin.

It was a beautiful warm day, and we talked for hours, consuming many a bottle of beer over the duration. I told him everything about my experience in Vancouver and my coming out. He said he was happy for me because I could live an honest life. He admitted that he had always known and that is why he had kept tabs on me over the years. As the evening faded into the night I was well and truly drunk and I didn't care. I wanted to ask him everything about being a gay man because I felt safe in his presence. He offered to cook me dinner at his place and an offer of free food is one I never turn down. I accepted, hoping that it might lead to even more exploration in private.

He cooked pizza and I had water. I was feeling relaxed at this point rather than drunk. The evening hit that awkward point after food and I found myself sitting opposite Matthew on the couch. It was getting late and I had to decide whether I was going to stay or go. Matthew, being the amazing gentleman he is, left it up to me to decide and I said I would stay.

"What do you want to do now?" he asked. "I have some DVDs here if you like?"

"I'm good," I said back to him.

"We could try kissing," he suggested.

I was curious and ready for something to happen so I agreed and at approximately 10:30 pm on March 21, 2010, I had my first gay kiss. By candlelight no less. It was nice and gentle and safe; in other words, the perfect first kiss.

Before we got any further than kissing, I wanted to text home to make sure Mum didn't worry if I didn't arrive home that night.

Hi Mum, crashing in my friend's tonight. See you in the morning :)

She texted back: *Are you ok? Who are you staying with?*

Matthew. We met for drinks today. I'm fine just tired.

A few minutes later: *Just be safe. I'll talk to you tomorrow.*

I threw down the phone and we moved to the bedroom. Now,

I am not going to go into graphic details here because, honestly, it was all a bit of a blur. The first thing to say is I am grateful that Matthew was the one I was with. He was kind and generous. He put me at my ease. Secondly, even going this far with a man confirmed to me that I was indeed gay. Kissing him felt right even if I had no idea what I was doing. I had never felt any type of Catholic guilt about being gay and had watched a lot of gay porn in an attempt to educate myself on all aspects of copulating with men. Now that we were here, rapidly getting naked, I was torn between running away and letting loose. I had nowhere to run so letting loose seemed like the sensible thing to do. I wanted to impress Matthew and the fact that he was experienced made the whole night feel a little one-sided.

Thinking back to that night, a term from the TV show *Buffy the Vampire Slayer* keeps coming to mind: angry puppy. That is what I was like in bed that night. There was a lot of noise, rolling around and groping about but ultimately very little actual progress or love-making. Matthew told me that there were things I wasn't ready for yet and I felt hurt. *You don't get to tell me what to do!* I stopped what I was trying to do and lay up on my side. He could see I was hurt and just said, "Relax and stop trying so hard. Everything is fine." We kissed again and, over the next hour or so, we got the job done. I fell asleep in his arms.

The next morning, I awoke to a sore head and a severe case of dehydration. Matthew needed to go to work so I had to take the tram home. As we were leaving, he asked me if I left anything in his room.

"Just my virginity!" I said and burst out laughing.

He looked shocked and not impressed with my quick wit. He repeated the question again with a slightly harsher tone. I took the hint and said that I had everything and that I would text him later.

I smiled all the way home on the tram, with a bad case of

bed head and the lingering scent of alcohol emanating from my person. For others it might have been a walk of shame, for me it was a walk of victory. I wasn't going to die a virgin. As irrational as it sounds, it had become a real fear of mine.

Arriving home, Mum summoned me into her room. I stumbled up the stairs and found her in her room. I raised my hands and said, "Everything's fine. Trust me."

I sauntered down the stairs, being careful not to fall, and into the kitchen to make a cup of tea. I was surprised by how Matthew's scent lingered on my skin. Having a shower helped wake me up and the feeling of relief stuck with me. Later that day, Mum took me for lunch. As I sat there eating a burger, she said that she wanted to talk to me about the other night: trapped, like Ripley on the *Nostromo* being stalked by the alien. I had fallen right into my mother's snare, but it wasn't a trap. Mum didn't make a scene or ask me anything too personal. She'd read the writing—or rather text messages—on the wall.

"Be careful. Take your time. Don't jump into anything." She even said that I deserved to be happy and that she was proud of me. Good mother advice.

Crazily, Matthew and I began dating, seeing each other at weekends; while I liked him, I had no idea what to say to him, let alone how to feel about him. We had a love of science fiction and attraction on our side but I was feeling a little smothered, if I am being honest, and I wasn't looking for a boyfriend.

One weekend my parents were away and I invited him over for dinner—my turn to cook for a change. When it came to where he was going to sleep, we had a problem. There was only a single bed in my room, and I wasn't going to let him sleep on the couch and certainly not the floor. Jenny and Susan's rooms were both vacant, since they had long since left home. I decided on Susan's bed, which was in fact Mum and Dad's old one. Nothing happened that night: we stayed up late watching old episodes of *Doctor Who*, the BBC sci-fi series. In the morning, I cooked him breakfast. My culinary skills are rudimentary, but he didn't get sick or die and then he went home. It was a nice stress-free night. I met Dean and Leon the next afternoon to go to the cinema, but throughout the movie I felt uncomfortable. It was guilt. Matthew had stayed overnight in the house and I hadn't asked for permission. Guilt rapidly morphed into panic. *What if the bed we slept in smells of man?* I began to get really nervous. *Will Matthew's scent be on the bed or in the house like it is on me? Will Mum or Dad find out? Will I be in trouble?*

As soon as the movie ended, I ran out of the theatre. "I've got something I've got to take care of," I shouted at my startled cousins' faces. I drove home like a crazy person. Running upstairs, I grabbed all the bedding off Susan's bed. If I had I been thinking rationally, that would have been enough. But, no, I convinced myself that the duvet and pillows would also smell of man. In a panic, I believed my parents had now Wolverine-like smelling abilities: I was going to be caught and punished for sure. I knew stuffing the duvet into the washing machine wasn't a great plan but I did it regardless. *I must clean it all!* I turned on the machine and went into the kitchen and waited. I was freaking out. I had ten cups of tea (really), which did little to settle my nerves, and went out to check on the machine every couple of minutes. What if it flooded the utility room because it was overloaded?

When the cycle was complete I took the duvet out and now it didn't smell of man. Oh no, it was dripping wet and stank of damp. It wouldn't fit in the tumble dryer and the rest of the bed sheets were all streaked with black rubber. I had ruined everything! I was nearly crying as I hung the duvet on the washing line and tried to dry it with a hairdryer. The sheets, however, were beyond hope.

I went into damage-control mode. Taking a picture of the sheets and ripping off their tag, I put the sopping wet stinking mess in a black bag and threw it into the boot of my car, like a murderer stashing a dead body. How I expected to get away with this, I don't know, for there was video surveillance covering the whole driveway. The evidence would be there for Mum to find. (Dad had once caught Susan sneaking home drunk this way so there was a precedent.) I jumped into the car and drove to the nearest Dunnes Stores.

I bought sheets that were the closest match I could find within my budget. And a new duvet too. It felt lighter than the one I'd destroyed but the clock was ticking; my parents would be home soon. Back the house at 5:30 pm, I ran upstairs, replaced the bedding and checked for any clues. Bedroom door open, as it was always open. Washing machine clean and smell-free. Ruined bedding hidden in the boot of my car (take to dump tomorrow). My deception was complete. Now all I had to do was play it cool and act normal.

Like any good criminal, I was going to use distraction and disinformation to put my parents off the scent. When they arrived home they found me playing a video game in my room. Dad asked me how I had gotten on—I lied and said I was having a nice weekend just chilling. Mum, being a little shrewder, asked if I had gone out at all? *She knows something is up!* No, of course not, I said and went back to my game. Home free, I thought.

About a week later, Mum walked into my room carrying a Brown Thomas bag. Unlike Dunnes Stores, Brown Thomas is prestigious and expensive department store in Dublin's city centre. I was surprised. Was it a present?

"What's in the bag, Mum?" I asked her.

"Sheets for your sister's bed."

Oh, crap!

"I don't know what happened," she said. "But I don't want strange men in the house, so you're going to invite Matthew here so I can meet him."

As this wasn't an unreasonable demand, I wasn't going to lie or protest. A line had been crossed and we both knew it, but she was letting me off easy. I had never brought anyone home before, girl or boy, so this was an issue that had never come up. I felt like an idiot and trapped living at home. Coming out late meant I couldn't skip steps, but that didn't mean I would like taking them. Over time, I came to realize how amazing and understanding my mother was really being. She knew I had to go through this process and I knew she had my back, just like when I went to Vancouver without selling the M3.

A week after the eventful encounter with Mum, I was doing some lesson planning in my dad's office, as I had begun working again at the English Language Studies Dublin (ELSD) school, when I received a phone call. The USIT operator congratulated me on the success of my application for a working holiday visa, which I had forgotten about. There were just under a thousand people in front of me, but somehow I had managed to get a year-long working holiday visa for Canada.

The woman on the other end of the phone was ecstatic for me while I was dumbfounded. "You can accept right away," she urged. Did I want to take up the visa? I had sudden flashbacks to my final night in Vancouver when I had rather obnoxiously told people I was gay, thinking I would never see them again. If I returned to Vancouver, how would I face them? The bigger issue was, did I want to go back to Canada? She could sense my hesitation and continued, "You can take a few days to think about it and let us know but you must decide within the next two weeks or the visa will be offered to someone else."

"Th-th-anks," I stuttered. "I'll be in touch soon." I put down the phone and just stood by the photocopier. My breathing was all over the place. I hadn't really stuttered since I'd been home. In fact, I had stuttered less. The idea of going back to Vancouver knocked the wind out of me. Even though I was making a bit of a mess of being gay, I was home and supported. Yet, I had spent a fortune on acting school and now had a chance to explore the acting scene as well as being gay in Vancouver, one of the most accepting cities in the world.

Restless and agitated, I locked up the office and went for a drive, eventually finding my way to Nana O'Brien's house. I burst into her home and excitedly told her my news.

"Nana, I've been offered a working holiday visa in Canada."

"Why, Rob, I'm thrilled for you," she exclaimed.

"I'm not sure what I should do," I confessed.

"Do you want to go?"

"Yes and no."

She looked at me and said something like what Mum had said when I went over to Vancouver the first time. "You only live once, and it is only a year. It is an amazing opportunity."

Unlike me, Nana O'Brien went to mass every Sunday and talked to God. I hoped she had his ear or maybe he had hers. This was going to be another leap of faith on my part. I didn't want to go. I loved being home; I loved having a car; I loved the safety of it all. But coming out had shown me that I had to start taking responsibility for my own life and begin to play a bigger game. Safety was in reality stagnation and it was only a year. Six more months than before. I decided then and there that I would be returning to Vancouver.

Deep down, I didn't want to go. My whole life felt like an act up to this point, so did I really want to be an actor? I didn't believe I had the talent or ability. My stutter was a huge hindrance that I couldn't let go of and, in some ways, acting and playing a part were the last things I should be doing now that I was finally beginning to figure out my sexuality. The next day I accepted the visa but deferred it for six months so I could save money and see where my embryonic relationship with Matthew was going. I rang him that night and mentioned the visa offer; I think we both knew it was over. We kept going for a week or two and then he called it quits over a lovely meal. To his credit, he handled it and me with real care and love. Some part of me was relieved. I didn't want to be tied down, yet I carried a lot of guilt about that, which would influence my future relationships.

Having spent my life savings on my previous stay in Vancouver, I focused on working to save as much money as I could. I scraped together about €3,000 between April and September, which is not bad on an ESL teacher's salary. Funnily enough, the idea of selling the M3 never came up over the six months, and it remained covered under a tarp in the hangar. I had my tickets booked for early September 2010 and, with money saved, I was ready to go. Amber, my acting coach, offered me a room in her friend's house so I now had a place to stay. All that was left to do was say goodbye and take the leap.

12

Looking for Stargates in Vancouver

The flight to Vancouver was the same connecting flight through Toronto with Air Canada and I knew what to expect this time. Immigration was slightly easier too as I had a working holiday visa but it still took about twenty minutes to print and place in my passport. I got my bags and went to the arrivals door. Amber was there with my new roommate, Dani. They were both excited to see me and we drove to my new home in Kitsilano. My room was a nice space with a large closet and mirrors along the walls. It was airy and clean if a little sterile. I was just happy to have landed and to have a bed for the night.

"What are your plans?" Amber asked.

"I will have to find a job and then look at taking acting classes and finding an agent," I told her. Inside, I was much more uncertain. To make the acting thing work, getting an agent was vital, as was finding a job. I had very little money (as always) and in the back of my mind was the M3. I had to make this a success or I would lose everything, including the Beast.

"Amber said you just recently came out," Dani said.

"Yes, six months gay," I said, smiling. I felt like I had failed at being gay too, as I remembered Matthew and the bedsheets. It was a funny story but it seemed only to reinforce my idea that my life was an absolute joke.

The initial week was great. I got to reconnect with a lot of my friends from acting school. I was in touch with home, too, using Skype and was feeling confident about finding a job. Paul, an actor friend, and I submitted ourselves for a showcase being held through VAS. As recent graduates, we qualified to audition and our scene was selected. We would have a few weeks to work on it and that allowed me to see Paul weekly, which was great. I also began looking for an agent, now that I was back in the country, and I hit pay dirt with a local boutique agency called Crystal Casting. I met with the agent, Klara, and she made it clear that I would have to continue training and be open to auditioning at a moment's notice. Being unemployed, that was fine with me and I signed on the dotted line.

In October, I turned thirty-three: still unemployed and feeling rather homesick. Another acting friend, Vivian, asked me over to her home, where she had a cake and T-shirt for me as birthday gifts. The T-shirt was printed with: "I don't kiss on the lips. Take it leave it or Fu*k Off." We had been talking about dating and I had shared that little opinion with her, which she thought it was hilarious. I have never worn the shirt out in public as it would beg the obvious question: if I don't kiss on the lips, where do I kiss? It was a lovely day and one I am grateful for because I was realizing that things were different. In being able to be honest about kissing and kissing men, I had made real progress, even if I was still struggling to find my feet in the city.

I had been looking for a job and sending out résumés but was having no luck. I didn't realize it at the time, but being on a working holiday visa made it harder to find a job as it was seen as a temporary status, usually held by young people travelling through the country. I wanted to stay in Vancouver, work and begin acting. Fun and travel weren't my priority. In addition, Kitsilano is a fashionable place to live, but notoriously expensive, my meagre €3,000 was depleting faster than a ruptured warp core. I discovered Vancouver is a town of contacts and networks and I had none; I couldn't even get a job in a coffee shop, because I had no serving experience (as a semi-fluent, non-native-English-speaking manager smugly told me with a polite smile on her face).

By November I was beginning to panic over money. Kitsilano was too expensive for me and I had to look for a new place to live. Another person came swooping in to my rescue: Rory. I had met him only twice before through acting friends. He rang and asked me over to his place to hang with a group of his friends over beer and hockey, a Canadian tradition. I said yes immediately and the night turned out to be amazing. I met a guy who worked as a stunt double on *Stargate Universe* and Rory's landlord was a sound specialist in the city who'd worked on various television shows and feature films. As the night wound down, I found myself alone with Rory on the couch and coming out to him. I knew he was straight and I hoped me being gay wouldn't trouble him. I really didn't know him at this point.

His response was unexpected. "Cool. I have a spare room if you ever want to move out of Kits," he offered.

I had mentioned over the course of the night that I was finding my current accommodation fiercely expensive but when presented with this opportunity, I hesitated. The room looked great and he would charge me about $400 less than I was paying a month. Why the hesitation? Simple. I was attracted to him. He was a great guy and adorable in a glasses-wearing, geeky kind of way. I was still hurting over Matthew or, at the very least, was unwilling to risk moving into a situation that might end in tears, my tears. I wanted to be safe and this felt very risky to me. I told him I would think about it and that I would keep in touch. I only half meant it.

That same month Paul and I put on our scene at the VAS showcase. It felt great to be back on stage but my stutter reared its head at the beginning of the scene. As I loosened up, my speech got more fluid. However, my nervousness worked for the scene as

Paul's character had chopped up my girlfriend and put her in the freezer. My character, John, had just discovered this and was nervously waving a fake plastic gun around in anger. We didn't win, but my agent Klara was in attendance and she was very happy with my performance. I wasn't. My fear of stuttering hadn't gone away and, now that I was away from my speech support network, I was struggling with it more than I let on. I didn't believe I could be an actor but couldn't say that out loud.

It didn't matter to me that much because by December I was out of money. I had paid my rent for the month along with my cell phone bill and transit pass. I had $20 in my account and ate tuna and rice for two weeks straight. I had sent out résumés to ESL schools in the city in a desperate attempt to find work. I Skyped Mum and Dad at the start of the month saying I had booked a ticket home in December and that I would be coming home for good. I felt so ashamed. As always, my parents were amazing and said it would be okay.

"Try and enjoy the last few weeks there, Rob," Mum said. Dad followed with, "I'll get the Polo out of the hangar again."

After I dried my tears and lay awake all night, the next day at 9:30 am I got a phone call from an ESL school, Hexagon IELTS School in downtown Vancouver. The woman on the phone, Lydia, asked if I had taught IELTS before. I had in Dublin for a few months and I was invited into the school for an interview. IELTS stands for the International English Language Testing System. Foreign nationals who want to study, work or immigrate to Canada must take this test. The interview was quick and informal and I was given a written task to work on for the second interview, which was the following week. I took this as a sign of hope even though a part of me really wanted to go home. The next week I was offered the job and, after a week of paid observations and trial lessons, I began teaching at Hexagon. I had a few days before my flight home and I earned my first $500 in Vancouver. I just about managed to cover my rent and food bills. I booked a return flight to Vancouver and was given ten days off to go home for Christmas.

Sitting at the airport, I looked back over the last few months. I had a job, an agent and a lot of possibilities for 2011. The weather on the flight out of Vancouver was mild but Europe was engulfed in snow storms. Mum and Dad had warned me about them as Jenny and Susan had just arrived home a few days before me. I had booked my flights for December 23, right after my first week at work. I even brought my suitcase to the school and left straight for the airport after classes ended. I was flying direct to London and the flight was the customary ten-hour one. Enough time for two movies and a nap.

I was tense on the plane as we were told by the pilots that London was covered in snow and all outbound flights were being suspended. I had travelled so far and was so close to home. If I had not been able to fly out of Vancouver, I could have handled it but this was torture. I found myself among numerous Irish people at the customer service desk in London. It was now December 24, Christmas Eve. People were angry and some irate. I was just numb. The last few months in Vancouver had been more than taxing and I just wanted to be home. I knew that wasn't going to happen and I didn't know what I was going to do.

We were told there was a possibility that we could fly out on Boxing Day, but I would still need a bed for a night or two. I got talking to a few strangers and shared my story of being in Vancouver and flying home for the holidays. One of the girls offered me a bed in her old apartment. She wasn't living there but she had it until the end of the month. I didn't know her from Adam and I had images of being raped, murdered and killed in some abandoned shack but she was Irish and a country girl and something inside me said to trust her and take a chance. Her name was Trixie and she was a nurse in London, studying to be a lawyer. In a random case of serendipity, I mentioned that I was an ESL teacher and that I had worked in Dublin. It turned out that I had worked with her brother at ELSD for years! I hadn't known him well, but she and I both felt instantly more connected. That night I crashed in a cold dark room, terrified and hungry. The optimism I felt at YVR had long since abandoned me. I was upset but I was also surprised at myself. I had said yes to an offer.

The next day I phoned home and spoke to my whole family. Dad, Jenny and Susan were on their way to Nana O'Brien's and I talked to Mum who was home alone preparing the dinner. I fought back tears on both calls because I knew, if I cried, they would just worry about me and there was nothing anyone could do. Trixie and I ended up having a great day.

We crashed a private Christmas dinner party in her local pub, where she had some pull with the manager. He was her sort-of boyfriend. I didn't know or care what that meant but it did allow me to get fed and dance and have a whole new type of Christmas. This was why I went back to Vancouver, to have these experiences. People asked me if I was single and I told them I was gay, which resulted in more questions than I would have liked about dating men and sex as the night went on, with people getting more drunk. The truth was, I had no answers as I was only figuring it out myself. My second night was again cold and slightly less frightening but my flight was confirmed for the 26th and that morning, Trixie took me to the underground and I found myself back at Heathrow. Trixie and I still keep in touch every December and her act of kindness opened my eyes to the possibilities of saying yes to things.

Arriving home on Boxing Day, I had only five days of my vacation left. As I had only started work, I didn't feel I could ask for more time off and I needed the money. I was determined to wring every last minute from the few days I had. Dinner was amazing and the presents were nice but the comfort of being home was priceless. I went to our local church and prayed. I had stopped talking to God years before, but my experience with Trixie had had an impact on me and I felt spiritual, for want of a better word. I don't know why but I wanted to say thank you to God for that and to pray for the coming year. I asked for a sign. I didn't expect angels to descend from the heavens but I really needed something.

It came in the form of a Facebook message from Rory. He was wishing me a happy Christmas and said the offer of a room was still open if I wanted it. For the second time in a week I found myself saying yes. We agreed to chat about it when I got back. I felt duty-bound to get back on a plane as I decided to view this offer as my sign from a higher power.

Back in Vancouver, I gave my month's notice and began to count down the days until my move. I viewed the room Rory was renting to me again and met my new landlords, Simon and Sarah. They lived in the house above the basement suite. It was close to the Skytrain, the local transit, and my room was smaller than before, but I liked Rory and, as with Trixie, I trusted him.

On February 1, I packed the very few possessions to my name. Rory had a car and we got everything moved in one trip. My first night in the basement suite he cooked steak and we watched some cartoons. Seriously, here was a man who spoke to my heart. I was still attracted to him and we spoke again about any issues he or we may have. It felt familiar, like in high school with the guys I had hung around with. It was odd. I was familiar with the physical aspects to being gay, but the emotional aspects were much more confusing. I had very little in common with Matthew, and here was a man who connected with me in a lot of ways. Over the weeks and months we lived together, we settled into a nice friendship and trouble-free living arrangement. He worked odd hours and I would see him sporadically during the week. I knew when he got home to give him time to decompress and, after an hour or two, we could hang out and chat, maybe watch cartoons or debate if fictional hyperdrive efficiencies are based on power sources or emitter strength. I had never experienced a bromance before but I imagined this is what it would be like. Rory taught me more than he will ever know and became a rock for me in Vancouver.

By this time, I had settled into my teaching job. It was secure and I was even saving a small amount of money due to my cheaper rent. My acting career was not taking off at the same pace, though. I managed to book the lead role in a student short and this caused a major upset at work. My boss agreed to give me the time off, but only this one time. The experience was exciting as we shot in a bar downtown and in a local film school. This was the first thing I had done since the showcase performance and I wanted it to be perfect. I played a guy in his early thirties, who was going against the system and being tried for a crime he didn't commit. I had a great, but emotionally challenging monologue, which allowed me to use my own experiences to fuel it and all went well. I was concerned about my stutter but managed to hide it. My agent was pleased that I was finally building a résumé of work, even if it was unpaid.

My school was unwilling to give me any more time off to act, which was reasonable, to an extent. I was very brave in my first year in Vancouver and I remember quitting after not being given a day off to shoot a short film where I was again offered the lead. I typed my letter and handed it in and explained that I was here to be an actor, not a teacher. I would like to think I stuck to my guns, but the truth was that I was living hand to cheque and, when the call from the school came to come back to work temporarily, I jumped at it.

I was still very apprehensive when acting. My stutter was there, constantly taunting me, and I feared it. I told myself that I could use the money from work to take acting classes and eventually I would get over it. This was a compromise that Klara agreed to. She said I would still be submitted for acting roles but she would be very selective until I found a more flexible job. I began taking classes with Amber as she had changed schools and was now giving group scene study classes. I wanted to recapture some of the old magic and believed she would help me learn to be a better actor. Like at Trinity, this would give me time to figure it all out. I hoped to keep things simple but a number of new people were about to enter my life and shake everything up.

13

I think I have AIDS!

Aside from my stutter, another nagging doubt I had about my acting ability was the fact that I had lived a very sheltered life and lacked the experiences other people my age would have had. Yes, I had dated Matthew and was deflowered, but as I was now getting settled in Vancouver, I felt it was time to start dating again. One of our neighbours, David, was gay. Visiting Rory and our landlords for a drink one evening, he asked me why I was still single. *Mmm, let's see. I'm rather clueless, emotionally needy and picky.*

"I've been really busy recently just putting down roots in the city," I told him.

David offered to take me to a gay bar sometime. Sarah, my landlady, was shaking her head and mouthing "no" to me when I looked over at her. I chose not to listen. She wasn't gay, and I knew she was getting sex as the walls in our house were thin. I knew I wouldn't go into a bar by myself so it was agreed that I would go with David next week to Davie Street, the gay village in Vancouver. I knew of this area but had actively avoided it.

I spent the week getting ready for David to take me drinking and, as the days progressed, I felt angrier and angrier. I was tired of feeling guilty over Matthew, I was tired of being lonely and, most of all, I was tired of being good. Being good meant having a job and paying rent and keeping Klara happy and my school happy and even, to an extent, keeping Rory happy, as I was living in his home.

I wanted to break free of the feeling that I had trapped myself in

Vancouver. I was working very hard but having no fun. Well, that was going to change.

David led me by the hand into the Purge Tank, a gay bar on Davie Street, after he had asked me what kind of men I was into. I'd said hairy, which equates to "bears" in gay speak. Having very little myself on my chest and face, I harboured some serious hair envy. We entered the Purge Tank and I found myself in bear heaven. There were hairy men everywhere and within minutes I was downing beer. I told myself this was only recon: look but not touch. I was pure chicken bait. (A chicken is an inexperienced gay man, usually young and newly out.) I was newly out, but not so young. David pointed out a guy saying, "He likes you." I had no idea how he could ascertain that from just looking at him, but then I was already rather drunk. We walked over to "Big Bear" and his group of friends. I don't know who kissed who first, but Big Bear and I began making out right there in the bar. No introductions or pleasantries. I could hear David saying, "Oh, my God," and I was ecstatic. There you go, not so nice and innocent Rob. The kissing was great too. I hadn't been kissed like this in my life. Passionate and risky. After we stopped, I proclaimed that I was going home with Big Bear but I had to ask him something first.

"What's your name?" I asked.

"Brent," replied Big Bear.

Classy and sophisticated I was not in that moment and I liked it. We got into a cab and I ended up at his place for an amazing night. I had months of pent-up sexual frustration and Brent was more than able to take it. I liked feeling angry and I hoped that my night with this man would be like when I drove the M3 in anger: that sex would click with me, would make sense, feel good and be effortless. I had come out and dated and all that, yet I feared sex. I was insecure about my body and my techniques. Matthew was too nice to ever criticize me, but here, now, was a random hairy stranger. I barely knew his name and I tried to give myself permission to just relax and see what would happen. A lot happened, more than once too, if I recall, and by 3:30 am I was in a cab going home to Rory, having promised to call Brent the next day.

This was now early Monday morning and I had to be up for work in a few hours. I fell into bed and awoke to my alarm going off. I managed to shower and clean myself up but on my face and neck were multiple hickeys. I could have called in sick but decided going in looking rough was preferable to picking up the phone. When my students asked me what had happened to my face, I replied with the double entendre of "being mauled by a bear." I swear some part of me wanted to be fired that day. The job was stable but mundane and energy-sapping. To my surprise, my boss said nothing to me about it and I carried on with the classes.

True to my word, I phoned Brent and returned to his place the next day with wine, the beginning of a crazy week of passion. By the Saturday, I was sitting at home bragging to Rory that it was a relief to be sitting down watching cartoons with him and keeping my pants on. I thought I was amazing. This was something new. This was me learning what it was to be a gay man.

I dated Brent for the next few months and, even though he cared for me, we were not well suited. He loved to drink and smoke. I did neither. He lived in his world and I lived in mine. We had very little in common and that does not bode well for a long-term relationship. Brent was also much more experienced than me, but that was going to probably be the case with any man I dated; I went with it. My actions inspired Rory to begin dating and he quickly found a girlfriend who would spell the end of our happy existence together.

The one thing I have learned about sharing with roommates is that as soon as a boy or girlfriend enters the picture, things quickly change. Rory began dating Tegan within days of meeting, which to be fair was exactly what Brent and I had done. The difference was that Tegan began spending a lot of time in the house and this was difficult for me, as I felt my space was invaded.. I remember coming home from work one evening at about 5:30 pm and she was there waiting for Rory to come home. Rory was on a night shift and wouldn't be home for hours. I was annoyed and felt like my space had been invaded. Tegan was oblivious to this and I knew straight away that this was going to be an issue.

Brent had never visited me at home because I had a roommate, and that meant that I always had to travel to him, which took an hour each way. Now that Tegan was effectively my third roommate, I welcomed the escape to Brent's. But I didn't feel like I had a real home; I was a prisoner in one and a guest in the other.

I tried to speak to Rory about this issue and he said he would deal with it. He didn't. For my part, I was trying to be nice and understanding about the whole thing but after two months or so, I began resenting both Rory and Tegan, along with paying rent for a home I wasn't really living in. I spent more time at Brent's and that pushed us closer together. He urged me to move out of Rory's place and change jobs but what he didn't understand was that I was only on a working holiday visa and that limited my opportunities.

My boss had just insisted that I become officially qualified to teach in British Columbia, which meant taking a three-month course in teacher training and a cost of around $1,500. Any notions I had of moving out quickly vanished and I tried to justify the course and expense to myself and everyone else. It was the same course I had taken in Dublin, but part of being an immigrant in a new country means having to go through these motions.

Rory and I moved to the upper part of our house. It was pitched to us by our landlord as a deal but it was more a move of convenience. I couldn't afford to move out and I didn't want to leave the security of Rory's place, even if it meant living with Tegan. My rent went up and my new room was a wooden panelled box room. I did have access to the office space at the back of the house and I escaped there every night to work on my teacher training course assignments.

Our home was to become even more crowded soon after we moved upstairs. A friend of Rory's crashed on our couch for a period of three months. When I say couch, maybe blanket on the floor would be more appropriate. Couch-surfer Jimmy was a funny guy; I loved having him in the house for no other reason than he annoyed Tegan as he was a constant presence in the living room, residing as he did on his blanket in the corner. I will always remember the night in the house before my first teacher practice. Rory and Tegan had fought over Jimmy and I was stressing about getting a stupid lesson plan written for the next day. I went outside onto the deck (which had been another selling point of our move, not that I cared about it) and looked up at the moon asking for guidance or a sign. This living arrangement wasn't working.

My prayers were answered but not in the way I expected. Brent had encouraged me to join his local gym as it was close to his home and we could work out together. I ended up going more often than he did, three nights a week and on weekends. I was looking for any excuse to stay away from home.

One Sunday morning I got talking to the man at the front desk. He was a powerful, loud personality, in many ways like Brent, and I assumed he was a strong man with knowledge and answers. He turned out to be a psychic witch called Tyr and, after a few weeks of chatting, I felt secure enough to open up to him about my relationship with Brent and my living arrangements. Maybe I was sharing too much but I desperately needed someone to talk to and he was happy to listen. He found the weekly updates on my living arrangements hilarious and telling them made me laugh too. It was a ridiculous situation. He was more concerned about my relationship status, however. He knew Brent (as he was in the same gym) and constantly quizzed me on why we were together. I never fully trusted his claim of just being a concerned friend. On my thirty-fourth birthday, Brent threw me an amazing surprise party. That night, under the influence of alcohol and pressure from him, we had unsafe sex. I wasn't too drunk to not know what I was doing but I was too afraid to say no and I felt I owed him this as he had put so much effort into the party. I didn't sleep that night; even though he assured me that he was STI safe, in my heart I didn't trust him, even though he was my boyfriend.

The next day, I panicked and arrived home early on Sunday morning announcing to Rory and Jimmy, "I have AIDS!"

I have to give Rory credit for the way he handled me in this state. Jimmy remained on his blanket. Rory said that I was probably fine and that I should go and get tested on Monday at one of the free clinics that Vancouver had available to gay men on Davie Street. I tried to stay calm but couldn't. Sleep eluded me so I hit the gym. I needed to get active to rage against Brent and myself for being so stupid.

Tyr was at the front desk and he knew something was wrong. I burst into tears and told him what had happened. He had the same look on his face that Rory had—a mix of pity, anger and disappointment. I couldn't tell who it was aimed at and I was too emotional to care. Tyr knew which clinic to use and gave me the information and address. I worked out and spoke to him for about an hour after my session. He told me the chances of having anything were very slim but he cautioned me, saying that I should be careful and that Brent shouldn't be forcing me to do things I didn't want to do.

Rory said virtually the same thing to me that night. I didn't need to be told that again; I knew it already and I knew that

I was going to have to deal with this relationship. I just didn't want to.

That Monday, I was not present in any of my classes. I knew the material and I got through the day knowing I was heading down to Davie Street to be tested for HIV and checked for other sexually transmitted diseases. The tension I felt was choking me and I walked into the clinic and told the man on reception, "I think I have AIDS."

He looked at me and paused before saying, "Some of us here do too." I had no idea about STIs or AIDS. I knew unsafe sex was unsafe and he asked me why I thought I had AIDS. I told him about the Saturday night and how we had been unsafe. He asked if my boyfriend was with me. I said no, and then he asked if my boyfriend was STI free. I could only say, "He says he is."

I was now feeling shame on top of my embarrassment. The word boyfriend felt so disingenuous. The fact I was there alone made me feel even more idiotic. I was told that the doctor was busy and had to be led into a waiting room to have my information taken. And then I met him. The Hot Nurse.

He introduced himself as Adam and he said some other stuff I wasn't listening to. I had never been in love and perhaps it was the fear of AIDS and a slow painful death or just being alone in this place, but I swear to the Almighty, I fell in love the minute I saw him. He was dressed casually and sitting behind a desk. The ginger hair was the first thing I noticed and he bore a striking resemblance to Keith from Trinity College. Most of all, he looked kind.

I was shaking at this point, emotionally paralyzed and infatuated all at the same time. I gave him my information rather fluently, relieved not to stutter in front of him. He talked to me about a safe sex survey he was conducting and asked if I wanted to take part in it. He could have been conducting a study on the sex life of orange peels and I would have signed up. I explained my situation, telling him that I had to go into meet the doctor and that I would come back after that.

The situation got even more bizarre when I met Doctor Tom. He was wearing jeans and a ripped T-shirt that exposed his tattoos, with a generally dishevelled appearance.

Is he even a doctor?

I retold him why I thought I had AIDS and he pretty much laughed. "You can't have AIDS," he said. "You may have HIV."

Doctor Tom went on to explain to me that the chances of getting HIV were low and if I was with my boyfriend I should be fine. He also questioned why said boyfriend wasn't with me as he proceeded to draw blood. He then pricked my finger to take the rapid test for HIV, which was ninety-nine percent effective. He said I was clean and told me the blood work would take two weeks to come back. He then gave me a leaflet about a gay coming-out course that was six weeks long, which I scoffed at as I had already come out. Doctor Tom looked at me for a few seconds before saying, "I think you may need this course. It will help you figure things out."

Looking at the brochure, I saw the course was to be held in the local community centre, five minutes from Brent's place.

I felt relieved but still nervous. I wanted the all-clear: even though ninety-nine percent was a high figure, I was convinced that I would be that one percent who actually got AIDS. I returned to Adam's office and informed him that I was clean and Doctor Tom was sending me on a sex course. He looked bemused at this—I dread to think what he was thinking—but I signed up for his survey and was very excited by the promise of four meetings at three-month intervals.

Back at Brent's place, I told him about the course. He laughed at me, claiming that I didn't need it. I looked at my arm where Doctor Tom had drawn blood and it was covered by a little round

Band-Aid. I knew he was wrong. I did need it and I needed more than being belittled by him as well. I needed a sympathetic ear. I needed a boyfriend who would listen and understand. I needed someone like Adam. Brent cooked me dinner and we watched some television before I packed my backpack and began my hour-long journey home. All night, all I could do was imagine what Adam would say to me, or what Adam would cook. Poor Brent didn't know it, but I had already checked out of our relationship and I was determined to use this six-week course to break free.

I was excited to begin my coming-out course. I was hoping that Adam would be there giving it and I could revel in his glory all night. Unfortunately, we had two admittedly excellent gay counsellors who introduced themselves in our little room within the community centre. I found it unnerving when one of counsellors closed the blinds as the room was being set up to ensure we had privacy. *Is this going to be a good cop, bad cop kind of thing?*

My whole outlook on gay culture was so off the mark that a part of me assumed we could all be having a sex orgy in this room. Ron, the counsellor closing the blinds, was an older man with grey hair and a kind smile. David, the other counsellor was more youthful and energetic with a boyish look about him. I decided I was more sexually attracted to Ron, though he was a poor substitute for Adam. Ron and David sat down and I joined the four other men in the room to sit in a semi-circle around them. Two of the men were not out and a much younger guy was questioning his sexuality. I was the only out gay among them and felt rather smug about that achievement.

David asked us to say a little bit about ourselves and I shared my story as succinctly as I could, ending with my current relationship and AIDS scare. My speech was okay, which surprised me, and I appreciated this opportunity to share my story with professional gay men. That night we spoke about having sexual feelings for men and how we could or did handle them. I got to share quite a bit about my own experience and coming out in acting school. Unlike at home, I was able to express my fear, anger and uncertainty around it. Over the next six weeks, these meetings became the high point of my life. We talked about everything from sexual and emotional health to dating and choice. For someone who didn't think he needed it, I took a lot of notes.

Week Two was all about how to come out to people. Having already been there and done that, I shared my own coming out stories. The next week, we dealt with dating and I cautiously shared about Matthew and Brent. Specifically, how Brent and I had met and our relationship. I didn't want to blame Brent or paint him as a villain because he wasn't, but it was clear to the room that I wasn't happy. Truthfully, I was hurt by the whole sex clinic debacle. Even if he knew with one hundred percent certainty that he was clean, I'd been scared and, as my boyfriend, he should have accompanied me. Ron kept asking me questions until I admitted that and I went further to say that I needed him to be there. Brent was a great guy but he lived his life and you either followed him or were left behind. I had spent months following him to bars and clubs and I was bored and unfulfilled. Luckily, Brent never asked me what I was learning in these sessions and I didn't volunteer any of this information. My test results came back all clear just before this session, which was a huge relief.

Our fourth session dealt with asking men out and dealing with crushes. That night, there was only two of us in the room along with Ron and Don. I mentioned Adam and felt so exposed doing so. I assumed Ron and David would know him but I knew they would not share the information. I came clean and said I signed up for the course in the hope he would be giving it and how I found him attractive and kind. I wanted to be with him or someone like him. Someone I felt at ease with and someone I could talk to. Someone who was a friend rather than the more experienced mentor figure that Brent played in my life.

By the fifth session, I was gutted that this support would soon be gone. I decided I had to break up with Brent before we finished the following week. At the gym that Saturday, I mentioned this to Tyr and he encouraged me to do it quickly and come back to him to let him know how it went. I went over to Brent's place as it was only a five-minute walk from the gym. He was on the couch and I just let it all out. Speech-wise I was choppy and embarrassed by that, but I said I wasn't happy and even though I did have feelings for him it wasn't enough. He took it well, not getting upset or even getting off the couch. I knew him well enough to suspect he was hiding his feelings but he accepted it and said thanks and wished me luck and said he would check up from time to time. That was the end of our relationship.

I told Ron and David that I had broken up with Brent at our last session; they seemed happy and we spoke about the future. These sessions were free and I knew they would be starting a new six-week cycle with new people. I asked them what I should do next and they said just to get out there and trust myself more. I had come a long way and felt free but I still didn't trust myself. I missed Brent and his social circle and

I spent the best part of a month sitting at home with Rory, Tegan and Jimmy. Both Rory and Jimmy said that I should get back out there and that moping around the house was not a good thing. Unlike Ron and David or even Tyr, I wasn't so sure of their advice. Rory was effectively living with his girlfriend after a few weeks of dating and Jimmy was still living on a blanket. Technology was to prove to be my saviour in the form of Netflix. This was early November 2011 and December was only a few short weeks away, which meant a two-week trip home.

14

No going back and climbing a mountain

I flew into Dublin on December 23, getting a coach to Donnybrook and Mum collecting me from there. It was a Friday and I knew Dad's work would be busy and Mum was nervous about driving alone into the airport. The coach was the easiest option and, after two years in Vancouver, I was well used to hauling myself on and off such transport. I had two weeks to just rest and relax.

Our house was due to be put on the market for sale in 2012, and Mum and Dad told me that I would have to pack up my room over the vacation. My bedroom had been painted and new curtains hung in the windows, along with a new carpet. It looked fine, just not my room anymore. The person I had been for all those years was gone too, replaced by someone I didn't know. Rory's home and my room there wasn't my place either. I was homeless.

I looked around my former bedroom and it didn't look like I had a lot of stuff. I had cleared out things like televisions and video game consoles when I moved to Vancouver. Now I was left with a more difficult task: to go through what was left and decide what to keep and what to throw out. We had to go through the attic as well.

I began packing on Christmas Eve after going shopping at 6:00 am and visiting my grandmothers along with Dean and Zara. Leon and Jen had left for Australia and were not there. Rather than trying to undertake the task in one go, I decided to do a drawer or two a day and see how that went, beginning with the drawers under my bed. What followed was three hours of sorting through old school books, VHS cassettes, some old Generation 1 Transformers, sci-fi books and the laughable copy of *What Is Happening to My Body?* complete with handsome ginger man on the front cover. Going through all these items that defined my past was an odd experience. What was harder was deciding what to keep and what to throw out. The books and VHS tapes went. The G1 Transformers and *What Is Happening to My Body?*, I couldn't let go. Being still newly gay and single, that image of a handsome ginger man leaning against a tree gave me hope for my own future and happiness.

The next day was Christmas day and we Skyped with Jenny in Australia, then had dinner. It was a great meal but being home felt bittersweet. Susan loved her life in America; I tolerated mine in Vancouver. Things were changing. What could I do if I stayed? With both Jenny and Susan gone, I didn't want to be the one to come back home, to be the child who failed.

It took a week to sort and pack the things I wanted to keep. I kept as little as possible to make the transportation of everything down to the hangar easier. I took some boxes in 98-D-1333 and Dad followed in his truck. He didn't cover my remaining possessions in the back of the truck saying it wouldn't rain. Like he had control over the weather or something.

We got down to Wexford in record time, and ten minutes later it began to rain. I unpacked all my boxes before finding a corner in the hangar to claim as my own. Half of what I kept consisted of video game consoles ranging from the original PlayStation launch model from 1996 to my Nintendo Wii, the last console I bought in Ireland. There were games and joypads all stored nicely in boxes.

"Why are you bothering to keep all these machines?" Dad asked me. "I hope they will be worth money someday," I replied.

The truth was that I have always had a fantasy of having a man cave-like home where I could display these machines in glass cases.

I still hadn't figured out how to find a profession where I would have the money to be able to afford a man-cave but I had hope.

Some books and two printed copies of my academic thesis on the Mini launch, which would eventually be published in early 2017, went on top of the consoles. Finally, models of the USS *Enterprise* (NCC-1701-D) and the USS *Defiant* (NX-74205) topped the stack like icing on a cake.

I had cleaned out my room and the attic and this was the result. All that remained of my life in Ireland was now a pile of games machines, books and two model starships. Seeing them all there was a sad thing. This was all I had to show for the thirty-four years of my life. More than that, I now had no room or home to come back to. It was all gone and nothing would ever be the same again.

I could feel the Beast's presence in the hangar too. I had avoided the M3 on purpose and it was still sitting in another corner covered and silent. It didn't feel silent to me. I felt a weight on my heart. What about the Beast? I had promised to sell it if my life in Vancouver didn't work out and I didn't think my life was working out at all. I had just packed up my old one and feared going back to my new one. I hadn't done any acting over the last twelve months, I was as broke as always and felt more alone now than at the beginning of the year. My residence status in Canada was still dubious, now that I was on a second one-year working holiday visa. At this rate, I would never amount to anything. The Beast would be sold and I would have failed in life, again. I had to commit to Vancouver and play big if I was ever to become the man worthy of the M3.

The next morning, I was on a plane back to London and from there to Vancouver. I got into YVR at about 6:30 pm local time, jumped on the Skytrain and, after an hour, was back in my room at Rory's. Tegan was over, cooking something in the kitchen beside my room. After only a few hours back it didn't feel like I had been gone at all. The next few months passed with very little to note. I had big plans and no idea how to achieve them. Work was the same mindless cycle of mundane teaching, class after class, and I was growing more annoyed with my living situation as the weeks went by. I couldn't afford not to work or move out as the Christmas trip home had exhausted my funds, but I could sign myself up on a dating app and maybe begin taking action on that front. I began chatting to a guy called Rudy, who was to be boyfriend Number Three.

Rudy lived on Davie Street and loved snowboarding. We chatted through text messages over the next few days and things moved rather quickly when we met towards the end of the week, on a Thursday. We made the mistake of going for beer. Now, I get drunk after two beers and, here in Canada, pitchers are dangerous things.

Meeting Rudy was like meeting a friend. We had common interests and the conversation was much freer than with Brent. That is not a criticism; he was just someone who I could geek out with. Rudy was a huge *Battlestar Galactica* fan and we talked about it for hours. I was still feeling vulnerable after my experience in the clinic, my break up and my crushes. I told some of the story about Adam and his sex survey as I was due to meet him the next week for my first of four scheduled meetings over the year. Rudy seemed kind, like Adam, and that was very attractive to me as we drank our beers.

I was amazed at Rudy's ability to drink—he was my size and was showing no signs of intoxication. Wanting to look good, I tried to keep up with him and ended up on the floor by the end of the night. Rudy said he lived around the corner and, in my drunken state, I assumed was about to get lucky. He walked me home, gave me a glass of water and we sat on the couch. I took the opportunity to pounce on him. He kindly pulled me off and said he didn't want to take advantage of me while drunk.

Really! I don't mind. Please feel free to take every advantage you want with me. I've been out of action for months.

Feeling the need to vomit, I jumped up and began heaving into his toilet. Not my finest moment. He ordered a cab, took me home and put me to bed. The house was empty and Rudy tucked me in before he left. I have no idea what I said to him but that act of kindness was something I had never experienced before. It was nothing like I expected and I remembered something the counsellor, David, had said: that people who are kind and don't take advantage are worth getting to know.

The next day, I phoned him and apologized for what happened. It was not an easy phone call to make and I was shocked when he asked me out to a going away party the next night. I had already made the decision not to drink for the obvious reasons and it was Rudy who ended up blind drunk that night. Our positions were reversed and I carried him home and put him to bed. Feeling lazy, I jumped into the bed beside him and the next morning, after a little fumbling around for a few hours, we officially began dating.

He was the polar opposite to Brent. Where being with Brent was hot and heavy, this was softer, kinder. I didn't feel the same pressure to perform sexually and Rudy was just plain adorable. Dating him was a great experience, and I still argue I got the better half of the deal. He cooked amazing meals and we could sit and chat for hours.

By mid-May in 2012, we had been dating for about two months and the skiing season was about to end. Rudy wanted to take one more trip to Whistler to go snowboarding. He asked me to come along. I had never skied in my life or felt the need to learn but this was my first trip out of Vancouver and I was more than excited to go on a weekend away with my boyfriend.

I remember this trip for another reason. I began my Permanent

Residency application after my school agreed to sponsor me. It would mean no acting for the eighteen-month duration of the application and keeping the same job but, along with being with Rudy, this was the progress I was looking for in my life. I met my immigration consultant hours before going to Whistler.

Rose was a beautiful wispy woman who exuded professionalism. She felt I had a good chance of being successful in my application. We outlined the steps I would need to take and she gave me hope that I could settle in Canada rather than living with the constant uncertainty I had endured with the temporary visas. Her services didn't come cheap but I felt secure and happy for the first time in the two years I had been living in Vancouver. She asked me about my bag and I told her about Rudy and our trip and how it was my first weekend away with my boyfriend! We joked that maybe I could marry him and skip all this visa nonsense.

That night in Whistler Rudy and I shared a few pints of Guinness and had a lovely meal. Going to bed that evening I felt I was dreaming. At last, things are finally happening.

The next day, I faced the mountain. Having no training whatsoever, Rudy assured me skiing was a simple art. Wanting to impress him, I followed him up the gondola and after the briefest demonstration of the "pizza" and "fries" ski positions, I was prepared to pull off. Now for those of you who don't ski, "pizza" refers to inverting your skis to make a pizza slice shape, which in theory slows you down and "fries" is where you open your skis, which speeds you up. It seemed ridiculously simple to me but, as toddlers on skis went buzzing past, I figured, why not?

Having no real control, I tried to keep my skis in the pizza position. That was great for about ten minutes, after which my calves and legs began to ache. I was flying down the mountain faster and faster. The only way I could stop myself was to deliberately fall down, which was great too, for about ten minutes, after which having to constantly pick myself up became exhausting. Thirty minutes later, I was done, but I had only reached the first way-point on the journey down. Still not wanting to lose face, I kept smiling and told Rudy everything was fine. Then I fell off the ski lift and saw that people were laughing at me. "Rudy, is there any other way down the mountain?" I asked. "I'm done, I'm sorry."

There was no other way down the mountain and poor Rudy had to demonstrate his snowboarding skills by guiding me down backwards. He held my ski poles and we slowly made our way down. I was exhausted and wanted to cry. *Don't leave me here!* Despite that, it was a beautiful experience because I was being vulnerable with this man in a very non-sexual way. After what must have been over an hour limping down the mountain, we made it back to the hotel. I bought Rudy a steak that night and soaked in a hot bath before going to bed drained.

The next day, he went snowboarding alone and I got to explore Whistler, the main skiing resort in British Columbia. I found a foreign food store where I bought some Heinz baked beans and bread for the kitchen in our the hotel room. Rudy got back in the evening and we just chilled out in the room. The weekend had been amazing and my first real trip outside of Vancouver. I now considered Rudy my boyfriend and having to trust him was a massive step in my development. I didn't trust most people but I trusted him.

Rudy wouldn't take money from me for the hotel room as he insisted he would have been in the room alone anyway and had some kind of special deal regardless. That was another thing I appreciated about him: he had his own car, home and job. He was self-made and independent and, in my eyes, very successful. As a foreigner on a temporary visa with wild outlandish dreams and a tiny bank account, I felt so beneath him in a real-world sense. I wondered when he would figure out that I wasn't the catch he saw me as, but I knew he wouldn't figure it out that happy weekend. Happiness was something I wasn't used to feeling very often. I told myself that everything would be fine once I got my permanent residency because then I could change jobs and really explore acting as a viable career. I would have legal status and be able to claim basic benefits and most of all, I would have some choice in the matter of staying or leaving Vancouver.

The drive back to Vancouver was quick. Rory was home with Tegan and they were cooking in the kitchen. Jimmy was on his blanket tapping away on his laptop. I didn't ask Rudy in as he had to pick up his dog which let me off the hook. I promised to have him over the following week. Jimmy was going to be out with friends, Rory would be working and Tegan had a family trip planned. I would be alone in the house. Rory made a big deal about me having a boy over to stay in the "Princess" bed. He had been working on a show called *The Secret Circle* with a mainly female cast and had gotten my girly-girly bed frame off the set when the show was cancelled. Thankfully, it was beige and not pink, but the bed had structural issues and wasn't the most stable thing in the world, as Rudy was to discover.

I cooked a simple chicken dish for Rudy, after Rory had assembled all the ingredients and let me prepare it as my own. After dinner, I showed him my bedroom, nasty as it was, and told him to come over and sit on the bed. I wasn't trying to lure him in for some hot and heavy action. Yet. We still had dessert to go and a movie to watch. As soon as his butt reached the mattress, the supports gave way and the bed partially collapsed.

"It's not my fault," he shouted

I laughed though I was disappointed: this bed would be seeing no action that night. The rest of the evening was a little odd. Even though I lived in this house it wasn't really mine. I lived mostly in my room and sitting in the living room watching a movie on

Rory's TV felt weird, while Rudy was embarrassed over the whole bed thing. Rory came home while Rudy was still there and got to meet him for the first time. He had never met Brent so this was new territory for both of us. I valued Rory's opinion and it was important to me that he liked Rudy. They were polite to each other and then, being a mean tease, I said, "So, Rudy broke the Princess Bed."

I know, I know. I do not deserve to find happiness with any man. Poor Rudy was mortified, but Rory said, "It's no big deal. I can fix it easily." Which he did, the following day.

I was discovering that dating Rudy was very different to dating Brent. Having him over that night really made me appreciate the fact that I needed and wanted Rory's approval and that having someone over to my home made me vulnerable. The fact that Rudy had come over in the first place made me appreciate him even more.

15

From joy to despair and it is all my fault

The greatest thing about dating Rudy was that it was the first relationship that felt real. We did ordinary things—walking his dog, hanging out and, on one occasion, replacing his toilet. Things were going well for us and, while celebrating Canada Day 2012 at home with Rory, Tegan and Jimmy, Rudy arrived with steaks and beer. Rudy loved steak and so did I. This day was the first time he officially met everyone living in my home. It was a relaxing, laid back day and towards the end we went back to his place. Susan rang me during dinner that night (yes, I was still eating) and it was odd for her to call. After making sure everything was all right, she invited us down to San Diego to celebrate Pride in three weeks' time. She sent me links to cheap flights, offered to put us up for free so we would only have to pay travel expenses— Susan wasn't going to take no for an answer.

Rudy was a frequent flier so for him this was nothing, while I was living pay cheque to mouth. Signing up with an immigration lawyer was costing me thousands of dollars so even flying to America on cheap flights was going to put me under financial pressure. A bigger worry for me was the border guards. American immigration can be a pain at the best of times and I was still on my working holiday visa which was due to expire that October.

All of this paled before the big issue: I had never brought anyone home to meet the family. What if Susan didn't like Rudy? Would I have to dump him? The whole thing had me in knots of anxiety. Rudy was excited to meet my sister; I had shared some of her more colourful childhood antics and he was curious to put a face to the legend that was Susan.

Despite my reservations, we booked our tickets for July 20–23, flying into Los Angeles where Susan would collect us. Flying into LAX was easy; as we had no luggage, we simply disembarked and went to the arrivals area. Susan had told me to meet her outside and said she would be driving a Honda Civic. By this point I was nervous. Susan would be meeting Rudy. Rudy, my boyfriend. I wondered if she had thought about us kissing or having sex. I know it sounds crazy, but that is what I was thinking.

I texted Susan when we arrived and let her know we were waiting at the car pick up area. She arrived pretty much right on time. She honked the horn and ushered us frantically into the car. We jumped in. Susan was driving, navigating with her cell phone in her hand and trying to drink a fruit smoothie all at the same time. Rudy sat in the back and I was in the passenger seat. As we got onto the highway heading towards San Diego she put the phone down and began to relax. She turned to Rudy and said, "Don't worry about a thing, Rudy, we are all cocksuckers here."

Did she really just say that?

Rudy just said, "I can see how you two are related."

This was going to be an interesting weekend.

As we drove Susan began to warn us about her rescue dog, Eugene, a little white poodle. Very cute and cuddly but with special needs. He had been kept in cage as a puppy, had anti-social tendencies and he and his tendencies were at home waiting for us. I had never been to Susan's place in San Diego. She was still studying but only a year away from graduating from her doctoral degree. Her apartment was amazing, fully furnished with a TV and her own items scattered around. It felt like her home; it was her home. She seemed to have it all, except a boyfriend.

We introduced ourselves to Eugene and found a fridge full of beer. Susan asked Rudy how we had met and I hung my head in shame and let him answer with whatever he was going to say.

"I picked him up drunk in a bar downtown," Rudy explained.

I smiled as I knew it was only half the story. "And he then took me home and put me to bed."

After settling, we freshened up and went to dinner. It was some fancy Indian-themed restaurant that Susan was raving about and we got to meet a few more of her friends. It was great to hang out with my sister, who is a free spirit and free speaker. We went out dancing that night and then got home ready for bed. Susan kindly gave us her room but said, "No sex in my bed!" With her outside I certainly hadn't planned on there being any sex, but then I remembered Matthew and the bedsheet debacle and decided to let the comment go. I stripped down to my boxers and T-shirt and jumped into the bed. Rudy had brought pajamas with him that made him look like an old man and I laughed at him.

"What? It's your sister's place, I want to be respectful," he said.

I didn't appreciate the sentiment then but I do now. Pride was the next day and the weather was warmer than in Vancouver so I put on lashings of sun cream. For me Pride is Pride. It was fun and exciting, hot men everywhere and just a joyous atmosphere. Being there with Rudy and Susan and a group of her friends is what made it the best Pride ever. I felt like I was with family and being able to celebrate the day with my boyfriend made coming out worth it. We ate and drank all day, with both Susan and Rudy both able to outdrink me—nothing new there. We ended up in a park somewhere just chilling as the sun set. By about 7:00 pm, people were walking home and it was the first time Susan and I had an opportunity to talk alone.

"You seem happy," she said. "Yeah, I guess I am."

"It is good you came down here. I like Rudy."

That was a huge relief to hear. This was all new and exciting and made me feel like a normal person. I had spent so many years alone, having pushed people away, that having someone in my life, regardless of whether it was a man or a woman, was a landmark achievement.

The next day we were off to see the USS *Midway*. To see a real battleship excited my inner child no end. Susan insisted that we start in the bowels of the ship and work our way up. Since she was driving us back to the airport later, she was the boss. We started in the engine room and from there the hangar deck. People were free to walk around and there was a gift shop and restaurant at the end. Rudy has a thing for magnets so, as he and Susan were grabbing food, I popped into the shop and bought him a magnet as a souvenir. We had already picked up a pink inflatable flamingo the day before but this was a gift from me to him.

I joined them in the café, ate away and discovered I was nervous about giving him a magnet worth around $5. I knew it wasn't about the money. I wanted to thank him for being there with me and making the trip so special. Blushing, I turned to him and said, "Here, I got you something," nearly throwing the bag at him. I could see Susan smiling at me and this made me even redder but I knew she was just proud. Rudy was blushing now and said thank you. We hugged.

Susan, still smiling, said, "You guys are so cute."

We were late for our flight, with Susan on a mission to get us on the plane. Once again navigating with her phone, this time it was Rudy, who was used to driving at liberal speeds himself, sitting beside her. I just stayed quiet. I didn't want to stress Susan any more than she already was. There was no point. Whatever was going to happen was going to happen. We arrived at the airport with ten minutes to spare only to see our plane had been delayed for an hour and a half! We got back to Vancouver at 12:30 am. We were both ready for bed and I crashed at Rudy's that night, feeling that life was at last good for me.

The next few days were spent recuperating but I knew I would have to hit the gym eventually. I was still in the gym on Davie Street, which was an hour's trek from home. Walking to the gym, I ran into Adam. He was as handsome as ever and I was caught off guard. He asked me how things were and I asked him the same, a little more nervously. He asked me about my acting career, about which I had very little to say as my agent rarely contacted me due to my unavailability. Adam mentioned a photo shoot he was working on; they were looking for volunteers and my mouth volunteered me before I had even a few seconds to consider the wisdom of such an offer. He gave me the contact information and I skipped to the gym, excited about this new opportunity to be around him.

I told Rudy about the photo shoot as it was taking place the following weekend. He didn't really understand why I was doing it and I was beginning to feel something like guilt when I considered why I was doing it. The lifestyle shoot was focusing on healthy gay living and it was a good cause to be sure, but I was doing it for Adam. My crush on him hadn't faded; if anything it had gotten stronger. There was a visceral quality to it that I didn't feel for Rudy and that troubled me. Was I doing something wrong here?

The following week at the photo shoot, after spending hours getting ready, I found myself among many other gay men and a photographer. The actor in me was accustomed to all the lighting and set-ups, but the boy in me was quaking in his boots. Adam was there managing the whole event. I couldn't look at him in the face. I tried to feign relaxation but I just came off as awkward. I wanted to be able to talk to him, to impress him. He was perfect, very much like the ginger man on the front cover of *What Is*

Happening to My Body? I didn't know if these were real feelings or just infatuation. I had a great boyfriend and I was happy, but I had never felt feelings like this before. I Skyped home the next day at the earliest opportunity. I was hoping to get Mum at home to ask her a very important question. Dad answered:

"Hey, Dad, it's Rob. Is Mum around?"

"No, Rob. She is out."

"When is she home again?"

"Why? Is something wrong?"

"No, no, all is fine. I just wanted to ask her something," trying now to avoid being honest about my reason for calling.

"Maybe I can help?" Dad volunteered

Oh, God. I can't ask him this.

"Okay," I said. "How do you know if you love someone?"

There was a long silence and Dad tried to put on his sympathetic voice. "I don't know, Rob, I guess when you have strong feelings for someone."

He tried to elaborate and in the end returned to his original query. "Are you sure everything is okay? Is this about you and Rudy?" The mention of Rudy's name stung me.

"Kind of," I said. "I'm not sure what I am supposed to feel for him and I'm confused."

"Well, you should see what your heart says."

For Dad, that was a pretty profound and sweet thing to say. I appreciated he was trying to handle me in a gentle way and that he hadn't been expecting that question. We chatted for a while and, when enough time had passed, I let Dad off the hook, promising to be in touch next weekend, which was Pride in Vancouver.

After celebrating Pride in San Diego so recently, Pride in Vancouver felt like a repeat. Rudy lived very close to the parade route, which made things easier, and we watched the parade together.

I was still struggling with the love question I had asked Dad. Rudy made it clear that he wanted to settle down sooner rather than later and he was ready to commit. I wasn't. My visa situation was up in the air and I didn't know if I wanted to stay in Canada. More importantly, I didn't feel I had dated enough guys to really know what I wanted. To say nothing of the crazy feelings I had towards Adam or the lack of those very same feelings for Rudy. I had no idea who Adam really was, but I was drawn to him in a way that reminded me of Alan, Keith and even Noah. That was missing in our relationship. I wanted that with someone, especially someone I was thinking of committing to. Rudy and I danced around these issues over dinner, not really resolving anything.

August was coming to a close, with Rudy and I becoming more distant. When he asked me why, I said I was worried about my visa, which wasn't a total lie. My lawyer had submitted my paperwork and told me all I could do was wait. There was more going on. I was feeling trapped. Trapped at Rudy's and trapped at Rory's. Jimmy had been given until the end of the month to pack up his blanket and that left me without my buffer from Tegan.

One evening Rory found me sitting out on our deck. "It will be a quieter house once Jimmy is gone," he said.

"Will it be?" I asked. He looked at me and I just spit it out.

"Rory, I can't live in the house and pay rent if Tegan is here all the time. We both know that Jimmy has been a buffer."

Rory couldn't respond to that so I took a deep breath. "I'm moving out at the end of the month."

He looked sad but didn't say anything to stop me—we both knew why. Moving out was the last thing I wanted to do. I had loved living with Rory in the good old days when it was just us, but I knew those days were gone and I was on my own.

Rudy thought I had lost it when I told him I was moving out. It would be more expensive than living with someone, I had no furniture and no plan. He kindly said I could crash with him until I found a place and when I didn't enthusiastically take him up on his offer, he finally asked me what was going on with us. Backed into a corner I told him, "I really like you but I am not feeling what I think I should be feeling for you."

He looked hurt. "Okay, well, I don't really know what that is meant to mean."

I don't know if I was looking for help from him or understanding. I was struggling, really struggling, and he seemed to just not get it. I know what I was saying was hurting him and it was hurting me to say it.

"We jumped into a relationship so quickly," I continued. "I don't know that we want the same things." I was digging myself deeper and deeper and, after a few more minutes, I said, "I don't think I should stay here tonight." Rudy let me go.

On the Skytrain back to Rory's I began to panic. This felt like we were breaking up. I was breaking up with Rudy and Rory at the same time. I found a new place, a one-bedroom suite, that was close to the Skytrain and $150 dollars more than I was paying now. It was unfinished and the homeowner was doing most of the renovation work herself. This was the first time I'd had to sign a lease; by the end of the week, it was mine.

Finding a new home so quickly was a great relief. But I still had to talk to Rudy. He had been quiet over the week and I had been busy making sure this move would work. Walking to his house, I felt sick to my stomach. How things had changed in just a few months. He wasn't in so I walked down towards the park, where Rudy was throwing balls with his dog. He hadn't seen me, so I could have run away, but knew I had to deal with this. I waited for him to finish and, as he was walking up to his house, he saw me. Looking a bit surprised, he just said, "Hi."

JUST ONE MORE DRIVE

"Hi. Look, I need to be honest. I don't know if I can keep doing this. I know what I said last week didn't come out right but I am scared and with my visa issues, I don't know if this is fair to either of us."

"Are you breaking up with me?"

"Yes."

There was a tense pause.

"Okay. Well, thanks for everything, I guess." Rudy said. "Do you need to pick up any of your stuff?"

"No, I think I am okay."

"Right. Well, good luck with everything." And he walked away into his house.

And that was our break up.

The first night I was in shock. The next day I was in bits. Had I made the right choice? Was I mad? Could I take it all back or was it too late? In a moment of maturity, I chose to let it lie and see what was to come. If Rudy and I were meant to be together, then we would be. Packing was a great task to keep my mind busy; I only had my suitcase, few items of furniture and my princess bed. The next two weeks, leading up to the end of August, were heart-aching. It is funny: the things you miss when you are in a relationship. Rudy would usually send me text messages during work and they really lifted my spirits. I missed him, much more than I thought I would. I'm sure he felt the same but it was just another new thing for me to experience.

Rory helped me move into my new suite on September 1, 2012, and we got it done quickly. The suite looked nice, airy with white tiled floors and mirrors giving the illusion of being a larger than it really was. We moved the bed in and set it up. My kettle, floor mat and bed nightstand completed my inventory of furniture. No couch, no television, no carpet for the floor. I'd wanted to get out of a crowded house but now I was in an empty one with no one to share it with.

Rory looked at me sympathetically and I said, "Look, I can accumulate furniture as I go." We both knew that was me putting on a brave face. I was out of money with having to put a security deposit down and the idea of ordering furniture and having it delivered was something I just couldn't afford. I could have gone to second-hand markets and searched there but that still meant money. I would cope though; I had been through worse.

Things didn't improve as September gave way to October. After a month of living in solitude, Klara the agent called me. I knew from her tone it wasn't going to be good news. She said that she had to close the doors of the agency as there weren't enough people working, myself included. So ended my acting career, at least with her. Had it ever really started? If I am honest, the answer is no. I could have tried signing with another agent but not being able to work during the week meant I had little chance of signing with anyone.

On some level, I was happy that work was so inflexible. I was afraid to get back into acting because of my stutter. Put me on a real set and have "action" called and I would almost certainly block. I didn't want to put myself in that position. It stopped being fun even before our acting course ended. I hadn't been able to handle my speech there and nothing had changed since; I couldn't let it go. It was the reason I had boarded a plane in 2009 and the idea of being someone else now held a huge amount of appeal. Klara gave me her apologies and said she would put my profile on Vancouver's Casting Workbook as an "unrepresented" artist. I thanked her as I was grateful for her taking me on.

As October 17 and my birthday approached, I wished there was some way just to pack up, walk away and fly home. It was a lovely fantasy that was crushed by what should have been great news. Rose, my immigration consultant, phoned to say that my residency application had passed the initial and most difficult phase of provincial approval. I could now officially get my work permit and stay in Canada for the duration of my application. To get this news, on my birthday of all days: I pretended to be over-joyed for Rose's sake, speaking on the phone as tears streamed down my face. This was the only reason I had to stay, and now I was trapped in my teaching job for the next eighteen months. If I left, I would lose the application and my chance to become a Canadian resident. I had already signed the forms when she had submitted the application and part of me had hoped it would be rejected. Then I could return home having saved face. I could always claim I was sent home by the Canadian government and it wasn't my choice.

I sat on the stairs of the fire escape at work and took stock of my choices. It was my birthday; I had chosen to come back to Canada and to try to be an actor. I had chosen to be a teacher in this school. I had chosen to break up with Rudy. I had chosen to move out. I had chosen my new empty home. I had chosen to pursue this path towards citizenship. These were all my choices, and I effectively had chosen isolation and depression.

The next few months leading up to December 2012 were some of the darkest in Vancouver. Emotionally, I was devastated. At work, I felt nothing. Rory came over on occasion but it was not the same as before.

Even the potential promise of seeing Adam in November for our next interview didn't stir me. I was indifferent to the fact that he would be on vacation and that a colleague of his would administer the survey. I was too numb to even worry that Adam may be passing me off on someone else because he had figured I was a crazy stalker. It just didn't matter to me, nothing mattered. I sleepwalked through everything, gorging on jelly beans, tea and

Netflix, watching episodes of *Star Trek: The Next Generation*. The gentle thrum of the Enterprise's warp core was the only thing that brought me any kind of solace. Amidst all this, I had to get ready to put on my greatest performance yet, as the big brother at Jenny's wedding.

Brother of the bride, father of the bride

16

I rev the engine and the Beast talks back

The flight home for the wedding, set for December 27, seemed to take forever. I feared it was going to be torture. Living alone had given me a lot of time to reflect on my life; I was seeing that it wasn't just about being in Vancouver or acting or breaking up with Rudy. I had spent my whole life running, trying to be fixed. Trying to be normal. But no matter how hard I tried, nothing ever changed. I knew I would have to put on a happy face for my family but didn't know if I had any energy left. I was so tired of pretending. I didn't even care that, as the eldest child, I'd always imagined I would be the first one to marry, to have a wife and kids. To make Mum and Dad proud and look great in front of the whole world. I just didn't care about any of it anymore. What was the point?

The flight home did take longer than usual as I had booked a convoluted route home through America and Paris, in an attempt to save money. I didn't realize I would be sitting in Paris for seven hours waiting for the connecting flight. I didn't care. I wasn't in a rush to get anywhere and I was alone. Jenny and Paudie greeted me at the airport and drove me home in 98-D-1333. Normally, I would be annoyed by someone else driving my car but, again, I didn't care. I feigned excitement at the wedding. Jenny had found love with Paudie and chastised me for being too sentimental and emotional. I guess I had learned something in acting school.

Our family home had been on the market for a year and had failed to sell. It made the wedding preparations easier and I slept in the place formally known as my room. Christmas Eve and Day came and went. We ate and were merry. Dad and I had some nice bonding time on the 26th after the wedding rehearsal, during which I learned that I was apparently going to be given a prayer to read in the church but had yet to see it. Always an ominous sign. Dad and I left the church to put up directional signs to the wedding reception, which was in the village of Lyons, close to Celbridge. The drive was quiet enough as the roads were not too busy. We hung the signs on trees and poles and went for food after the task was finished. I even had a few beers.

"So, how are you doing?" Dad asked as I took my first sip. I am not sure if he was worried or just starting conversation.

"I'm tired still and a little down, I suppose."

"Well, it will be nice to see Louise again tomorrow."

"Yes, it will. I'm really happy she accepted the wedding invitation."

"You'll find someone else, Rob," Dad said. "You just need to be patient."

Louise was to be my wedding guest at the big event. Rudy and I had spoken about the wedding and the thought of him being there with me was bittersweet. I would be lying if I said it wasn't gnawing away at me a little. I was grateful to Louise for coming with me because she was one of the few people I could really relax with. Susan was in the same boat, in that she didn't have a man at the wedding. Her best friend from San Diego, Missy, had come with her.

The day of the wedding arrived and I have to give Jenny credit—she had planned it all from Sydney. The make-up woman came and got the ladies in the family ready. Dad and I suited up. Jenny came down the stairs in an amazing dress, looking beautiful and elegant. Susan followed in her purple maid-of-honour gown. She also looked beautiful. It was my job to drive Dad and

Jenny to the church and, when we arrived, Jenny handed me a card just before we went in.

"Oh, here is the prayer we'd like you to read."

In all my not-really-caring mindset, I had forgotten about the prayer. I put on my actor/performer hat and read away. I was fluent and loud and did a great job. I felt a twinge of anger. *I can read here now but can't really be an actor. Stupid bloody speech.*

The rest of the ceremony went perfectly, just as we had rehearsed. The reception was splendid, in an old-world style dining hall, complete with real fires in the fireplaces.

Mum, Dad, Jenny and Susan were all at the main table along with Paudie's family. Louise and I were sequestered with some of the more eccentric and loud members of the O'Brien clan at a table further away.

Two of my many cousins, Lisa and Ella, were sitting at our table. I hadn't seen them in years as they had both been overseas and I realized that they hadn't changed a bit. They were awesomely funny and totally inappropriate, and this coming from me. The four of us were joined by Aidan, a doctor in training, and his wife Katherine, who are close friends of Susan. Our meal began with soup and, as we were all eating, Lisa asked Aidan, "What do you like most about being a doctor?"

Ella instantly screamed out, "Vaginas!"

Without missing a beat, Lisa added, "Yeah, he saw Katherine's and wanted more!"

The pair erupted in mad loud cackling. Poor Aidan and Katherine said nothing, and I turned to Louise who was looking at her soup.

"Did they just say what I think they said?" she whispered to me.

"Yes, they did."

As the night went on, I was relieved to be away from my family. I could hide out here and just keep smiling and let my cousins entertain us. Having to mingle and talk about life in Vancouver really brought home the fact that I had made the decision to go there. I was miserable and I saw no way out, but it had been my decision. That was the worst thing about it. I remembered having wanted to drop out of Trinity, but a lack of any plan prevented me from doing anything about it. I was still using the same flawed strategy: suffer until something happens.

I spent three hours working the room, dancing, smiling and checking in on Louise every so often. Then I had a blast from the past when a man approached me. Stephen and I had been class-mates at Grange Park. I remembered his name and face. He was one of the popular kids in the school and we had little or no contact but I still remembered. He was the boyfriend of one of Jenny's work col-leagues. At least he has gotten fat, I thought as we chatted. He had a good job and girlfriend and seemed happy but admitted that he had fallen down years before. I shared with him that I felt lost and uncertain about my future and where it was going. An odd thing to tell a stranger, I guess, but then a stranger is the only one I could say that to and not have to explain it. Just admitting that made me feel a little lighter. We exchanged pleasantries and parted ways.

As the evening wore on, people began to fade. Jenny, still look-ing amazing, mingled around the room and Paudie sat with his brothers. I went and sat with Louise. She was looking tired and ready for bed. I was also exhausted having listened to people talk-ing about jobs, buying houses and having kids. Successful people, the people I had grown up with, my peers. To have a secure well-paying job, to be able to apply for a mortgage was something I couldn't fathom. Being in stable long-term relationships where there was love and commitment. Again, I couldn't imagine that for myself. Sure, they envied me, my courage and freedom to leave home and live in Vancouver. But then only I knew what I was going back to.

Louise and I took a golf cart back to our room. When we got there, she asked me what was wrong.

"I just don't see a way out, Lou. I don't want to go back to Vancouver but I have nothing here anymore either. I'm just so tired."

I knew Louise knew what I was going through, as she was going to be moving to London in the new year to restart her own life.

"We will figure it all out in the end. Just be patient," she advised and fell asleep.

I lay there for hours and couldn't sleep. I didn't think I could figure it out. I had tried and, right now, even been home felt wrong. Everything felt wrong. I thought back to all my years of counselling and speech therapy and all the work, all the sacrifices I had made. For what? It didn't seem fair.

I can't speak for anyone else in the family, but the relief of the wedding being over was immense. The next morning I thanked Louise again for being there with me. It was like old times. She gave me a huge hug and said, "Everything will be okay, and next year is a new year."

"I hope you are right."

Susan and Missy had a few days left in Ireland and my sister had a breakneck whistle-stop tour of the country planned for her friend. Jenny and Paudie were not going on their honeymoon until they returned to Australia so they were planning on relaxing with their respective families over the next few days. Mum and Dad were in great form telling everyone who would listen about the wedding.

That left me, and there was only one thing I wanted to do. I wanted to go for a drive. I wanted to escape onto the open road and be alone in a car again. Radio playing, engine singing, and that glorious sensation of power, speed and control. I drove the

Polo down to Wexford, to the hangar and the Beast. I made an excuse about getting something from my pile of possessions.

Arriving at the hangar and opening the door to find the Beast, still sitting covered, made me feel even more like a failure. A car like this deserves to be driven on the open road. It mirrored my own life of wasted potential, eternally waiting for someone or something to save it. And the Beast was waiting. Waiting for me to figure things out, be a success and own it. The car was sitting here, waiting for me to become the man I needed to be to own it, run it, embrace it. I wasn't that man and I didn't believe I ever would be.

I closed the hangar door and pulled the cover off the car with far less care than I like to admit. Looking at the dusty vehicle in front of me just reinforced the rage that was building in me. Who was I kidding? This thing would never race again, let alone turn a wheel. I got into the car and put the key in the ignition. Dad had turned the engine over from week to week so I was confident that it would tick over. The car's cockpit looked so small. The indicator and wiper stalkers were spindly and weak looking. The control check computer that I was so fascinated by as a child looked antiquated and the seat still squeaked. This was all I was ever going to get.

I thought of Rudy, Brent and Matthew. All the men I had been close to and now they were gone. I was alone and I knew I would always be alone. Everything I had worked for was to find love. To learn how to be loved and to give love in return. I looked at one of Jenny's wedding photos on my phone, the one showing her leaning on her husband with secure vulnerability and I couldn't imagine ever feeling that brave, or happy. What did she know that I didn't? Whatever it was, the lack of it was killing me.

I threw my phone down in the passenger seat and turned the key. The Beast's dashboard lit up and the fuel gauge instantly moved to read a quarter-full. Another turn of the key and the engine began to tick over; after a slight hesitation, it erupted into life. That feeling of the engine shaking the whole car was still the signature M3 greeting. I should have been worried about the engine. I knew enough about the S14 under the bonnet to know that its only real weakness is that its timing chain tensioner is oil fed and needs time for the pressure to build up. Having the engine idling after years of inactivity could cause excessive wear and potentially catastrophic engine failure. But today, I didn't care.

The engine never settled and continued to shake the car gently. Revving the engine caused it to rock the front end of the car as if it were trying to tear itself away from its mounting points. The engine was eager to race, to pull the car along with it while I was ready to let go and sleep. It was probably less than five minutes, but I felt as if I had been sitting in the Beast for hours. My mind was racing and my emotions were flaring. Starting the engine felt like taking control of my life in some small way and it felt good. I thought of Jenny being in love and married, Susan being happy with her friend and of Louise looking forward to her move to London—they were living, they were doing something with their lives.

I revved the engine.

I thought about love and how I had never felt it. How I would never have a marriage like my sister's and the idea of living with that emptiness for forty or fifty more years was too much to bear.

I revved the engine.

I knew I was booked on a plane to go back to Vancouver and I imagined buses and Skytrains and rain and the incessant, mind-numbing labour just to survive in a cold alien city that I laughably claimed as home. The endless lonely days and the interminable nights alone.

I revved the engine.

I thought of the thousands of euros I had wasted on actor training over the years. My own life savings and borrowed money based on my determination to succeed with acting. The time, the effort, the sheer emotional burden of the training. For what? To run away and be someone else, anyone else, other than the man I was, now sitting here. I had spent my life running and where had it gotten me? An idle car in a closed hangar. I revved the engine.

I feared the stutter that would never go away. The stutter that dominated my every waking thought and breath. The stutter I tried so hard to control, suppress and avoid. It stopped me acting, it stopped me dating, it stopped me looking for a new job, it stopped me even breathing at times. I knew my technique and I knew that by using it I would never be fluent and normal. I'd be that guy who stutters. I hated it; I wanted it to be gone. The only way to make that happen was for me to be gone too.

I revved the engine.

I remembered every bully whose path I'd crossed. *Well done, lads. Here I am trying to die. Well done. You were right. You fuckers have won.* They tortured me for being who I was. They stole my confidence from me, they ripped my faith from me as a child and I had never gotten it back. *Burn in hell. Live lives of pain and loss.* When I died, I was going to find them and haunt them.

I revved the engine.

I saw myself as that little boy. Before all the damage. Sitting in the garden playing his new Star Wars toy, a *Millennium Falcon.* The toy was bigger than he was but he loved playing with it. Making warp drive noises and imagining jumping with it into hyperspace. Dreaming of a life of adventure and hope. I wanted that child back. I needed him back. I wanted to start again, to try to be innocent and free but that is not how life works. I had failed. I had failed myself and everyone around me. I wasn't an actor, I was a liar. I had even failed the Beast. It would never race under my hand. It would either rot here or be sold.

I revved the engine.

Finally, I remembered Dan, who had killed himself. How I envied him still. He was free. Free from all this pain and despair. He had planned his suicide well and had been man enough to see it through. He was more impressive to me now in death than he ever had been in life.

I revved the engine.

But no matter how much I revved, the hangar wasn't filling up with enough gas to kill me. It was massive—large enough to house several helicopters—and I cursed Dad and his need for big buildings. I cursed the Beast for only having a 60-litre fuel tank; smaller than your garden variety E30 M3. The meter had been reading a quarter full but now the needle was sinking closer to empty. I felt sick and not from the fumes. Despairing, I imagined *Stargate's* Samantha Carter sitting in the passenger seat beside me. She was in her *SG-1* Air Force uniform, a laptop propped on her legs. Looking at the chart, she turned to me and said, "Given the hangar's dimensions and the dispersal rate of carbon monoxide, along with the limited fuel supply and the necessary concentration needed to kill a human, I'm sorry, sir, I don't see this working."

She looked at me sympathetically.

I can't even kill myself properly! How pathetic is that?

I looked back at the fuel gauge and through the windscreen out into hangar. No fumes to be seen. I began to cry. Imaginary Sam was now gone, and I was alone in the Beast.

As I cried, gripping the steering wheel, all I wanted was to be hugged. My anger evaporated and now I was that six-year-old boy from all those years ago. I needed a hug, a hug from a man. It hurt too much to think of Rudy, and I didn't want to think of Brent. Adam? No, Adam was a fantasy and he would be horrified by where I was and what I was doing. The same feeling of shame surfaced when I thought of Matthew, Noah and Keith.

The person I imagined sitting beside me now was my imaginary

Gareth from my *Four Weddings* monologue preparation: grey hair, blue eyes, all of it. It felt right. I had imagined us in this car going on dates, maybe even using it as my wedding car. Here was a man I had imagined loving. Gareth was the closest I had ever come to being in love, the embodiment of the life I wanted to have. A life like Jenny and Paudie's. Gareth was the person who would know me and accept me, even now as I sat in the Beast at my lowest point.

"Why are you doing this?" Gareth asked me.

"Because I am sad and done."

"This isn't the way. You want love and it is out there, waiting."

"Fuck you. You are only in my imagination."

"You created me and those feelings. That wasn't just acting; it was as real as you could make it. This is not the way."

How do you argue with yourself? He was right. I had felt something in these scenes with him. The hope of love. The joy of acting. The freedom to fully embrace loving someone, even if it was a man. I knew the world, religions, governments, even people on the street would say homosexuality is wrong. For years, I had made myself wrong but right now all I wanted was love. The rest of the world could go to hell. I deserved this, I wanted this, I needed it.

I looked back at the Beast's fuel gauge again. Had it moved further down? At this point, I couldn't tell. If this worked and the hangar filled with fumes and I died in the M3, who would find me? I thought back to Dan. Yes, I admired him and envied him his freedom but what of the people he'd left behind? Gareth was gone now, replaced by Dan's mother just as I remembered her nearly twenty years ago.

"I found him," she said. "Do you have any idea what that was like?"

A parent finding their child dead was more than trauma, it was soul destroying. I knew if I went through with this, it would be Dad who would find me.

Now he was now sitting where Dan's mother had been seconds before. I saw anger and grief in his face.

"What have you done? Why didn't you reach out and ask for help? There is no need to suffer like this. Now it is too late and this is going to destroy your mother and grandmothers and everyone who loves you. Jesus, Robert, what do we do now? What do I do with this car?"

I looked away from him in shame. I couldn't put my family through that, but I hated them for making me responsible for their contentment. Did I have to live a despairing life, just to spare them pain?

I looked back at the passenger seat, now empty once again. I turned off the ignition and the engine died instantly. The silence filled the hangar in a way the fumes had not. I used the remote control to open the building's door and light streamed in as whatever gases had accumulated escaped. I sat there in my race car with no idea where to go next.

17

What are your plans?

It was getting late in the afternoon and I could see the sun setting. Leaning back in the Beast's embrace, contemplating my unsuccessful suicide attempt, left me feeling strangely peaceful. All the anger had been spent and my tear ducts had run dry. My breathing had settled and I was at peace in the M3. Turning off the engine had been a decision to turn away from death. Perhaps I might have found a hose and duct tape around the hangar if I'd truly been a man on a mission; there was still enough fuel in the Beast's tank to try again. But I didn't. I didn't want to be one of those people who regularly tried to kill themselves. I had tried and failed and now it was time to move on. I had no idea what to move on to, but the engine was going to stay off.

I didn't have any answers for the future, but I did have a deadline. Mum had planned another post-wedding dinner and I'd said I would be back in Dublin by 7:30 pm. I got out of the Beast and put the cover back on the car. I placed my hand on its bonnet, which was still warm. The car was still here. It was still running and that made me smile: like me, this vehicle was resilient.

The next few days were a blur. We were all going our separate ways once again and the day before I flew back to Vancouver I visited Nana O'Brien to say goodbye. We chatted over tea and she asked about Jenny and Susan and then about me.

"What are your plans?" she asked.

I had lost count of the number of times I had been asked that irritating, default question over the last two weeks and I was sick of answering. *Well, let's see, I was planning on being dead so going back now . . . well, I am drawing a blank. Sorry.*

We sat there in silence, and Nana was the first to speak. "You chose to go back there two years ago and you are choosing it now. You have control over your life and you are old enough to be responsible."

Had those words come from someone else they would have stung, but from Nana they were different. I listened to her. I felt I had no control at all—not over my life, my speech, my sexuality and certainly no control over what other people said and did. My grandmother then changed the subject and we chatted for another half an hour or so. Then I took my coat in hand, hugged her and thanked her, really thanked her, for what she had said. There was something there to consider. I had always told myself I had no control; yet in the Beast that day, I did have control. I had control over the engine and I chose to turn it off.

The last stop I had to make that night was to Nana Iremonger in the nursing home. Nana had made it to Jenny's wedding for an hour or so and, to my shame, I'd only greeted her and spoken to her for a few minutes. I could see that the effort of making it to the wedding had taken a lot out of her, and me not talking to her properly had been rude. This evening, Mum was with Nana, who was being difficult. I walked in and said hello and it took a few seconds for my face to register with her, but when it did, she calmed down and looked at me in a way only a grandparent can—with complete unequivocal love and pride, regardless of how I saw myself.

I stayed with her for thirty minutes or so and we chatted, allowing Mum to take a break. Nana was in her nineties and was repeating herself in a way I had never heard before; it gut-punched me that this might be the last time I'd see her alive. Losing her would mean losing another connection to my childhood, to happier times. Mum came back into the room and said, "You should go home, Robert, and pack for your flight tomorrow."

I went to hug Nana gently and said, "I love you and I will see you again soon."

"Goodbye, Robert," Nana said, giving me a look I will never forget. It was knowing, loving and peaceful. Maybe she, as well, knew that she would never see me again. That was the last time I saw her alive and her final look has stayed with me ever since. Nana saw something in me I couldn't recognize in myself. I wanted to see the man she saw. I wanted to live and fight to become that man for her and for Granddad. What if I could be more? First Nana O'Brien's comment about having control over my life and now this loving last look from Nana Iremonger. These women had raised me and they knew me. They knew the child I'd been and saw the man I could be.

Mum and Dad drove me out to the airport the next day. The flights back gave me plenty of time to think, even though they were more direct with no seven-hour layovers this time. What did I want and where was I going? The events in the hangar kept replaying in my head. Feelings, memories and thoughts swirled around me. The weariness is what I was drawn to. The innocent child playing with his toys is who I wanted to get back to. I wanted that freedom again to just be me. As an adult, driving gave me that freedom; that day I drove to Tullamore in the Beast was the best driving experience of my life and I wanted to feel that way again. I knew I couldn't turn myself back into a child but I could drive the Beast again.

During that flight back to Vancouver, the Beast became more than a collection of metal panels welded together, it became my aspiration for a better life. 90-D-41990 had done what every car in my life had done: it had kept me safe, especially on that day when I needed safety more than anything in the world. All my pain, all my broken dreams, all my hopes for the future—this car had cradled them and me. The Beast had protected the dreamer in me and had given me new hope. Hope for not just one more drive, but many more drives, drives which weren't just running away or hiding. Drives where I was embracing every last ounce of life. Drives where I could take risks, knowing that all would be well. Drives where I would become whole again.

Getting back to YVR, I felt strong and determined. This place wasn't home, but it was where I was choosing to be. My permanent residency application was a package deal with work. Both Nanas had given me separate gifts and the Beast was the prize. It was the beginning of 2013 and this was going to be a new year.

The initial week back was about getting a routine in order. I went to work and shopped to stock my empty fridge. Jenny had sent us her wedding photos, and while everyone else looked great, my face had a puffy look and hints of a double chin, so I decided to put real effort into hitting the gym again. I didn't think I had let myself go, but grieving Rudy and a diet of jelly beans and cups of tea had taken their toll.

Going back to the gym was a chore as it was just over an hour from where I was living and the trekking there had long lost its appeal, but at least it gave me a sense of control over my physical body. My Wiccan friend Tyr was still working at the front desk and we got chatting when I finished a workout. He said he had a room in his house in Kerrisdale, a forty-minute bus ride from downtown. I was paying $850 a month in rent and Tyr was offering a room for $500. I knew Tyr had a magic school in his home, which sounded crazy, but I wanted to live with other people again as I could see my isolation was not working. I accepted his offer, planning to move in February.

When the time came, Rory kindly helped me as it was a great excuse to hang out. He was now living in his own place with Tegan. Tyr's house was old and a little dilapidated but the room itself was very big and Rory was impressed. As we were moving my stuff in, Tyr was conducting his magic class in the room below. After all my joking about looking like Harry Potter in my Mini driving youth, now I was living in a real-life Hogwarts.

Living in Tyr's home was an experience: I was amazed that people were paying for these magic classes. I had no idea if he was crazy or an authentic wizard, mage, warlock or whatever the proper term was, but he would stroll up to my room with a pouch full of cash and say what a joy it was to teach magic. There were five of us in the dilapidated house, along with two black cats, and it felt nice to be surrounded by people again. We lived in an area of perfect homes in Kerrisdale, and our neighbour groomed the lawn in front of her impeccable home every day. The contrast with ours was like something out of a comedy horror movie.

This didn't bother me, as it was just a place to live and one where I could save money as my rent was effectively halved (thank you, Tyr). Both driving and gaming were still my passions; although I couldn't afford a car, I was now considering an Xbox. My original Xbox 360, one of the early white models, was sitting in the hangar in Dublin. Could I justify buying the same console in slim form here in Vancouver when I would be returning home eventually? It would be a waste of money.

I mentioned this to Tyr one day, to which he said, "You're crazy, man. Make your life as comfortable as you can." He was right. I didn't know if I deserved an Xbox but I wanted one and the next weekend it was sitting on my desk. I sent Rory and Jimmy a photo and they were amazed that I had finally bought one. I felt like crying as I held my joypad in my hands and played Halo 4, helping the Master Chief and Cortana save Earth. This was the first thing I had bought for myself in Vancouver that wasn't a necessity and it made me feel proud and happy, like a man who could treat himself on occasion. That was real magic.

18

The Geek meets the Queen

Tyr and his coven had monthly prayer ceremonies to the moon and they encouraged me to take part. This involved writing down promises to the new moon and burning them in a cauldron. At one of these moon ceremonies, a couple of the guests suggested that I take up acting classes again after I had casually mentioned what had brought me to Vancouver in the first place.

Work was so predictable that I could do it in my sleep; I was saving enough money on rent to be able to afford acting classes, so I considered it. Encouraged by the mystical power of the moon, I reached out to my old acting coach, Amber, who was now at a different school, the Vancouver branch of an American acting school called The Los Angeles Acting Institution, where they used a hybrid version of the Meisner technique to help actors be more natural in their scenes. There was an improvisation component that really allowed us to relax and play within the scene.

After talking to Amber and sitting in on a class, I signed up, feeling good to be back. I hoped that I had changed over the years and gained more experience in my life to bring to my acting. In the past, love, sex and intimacy had been alien concepts but being with Matthew, Brent and Rudy had educated me. I was also more independent, surviving in Vancouver, though my old stuttering fears still made me nervous about every class. I hated cold readings and every blip or block in my speech triggered me internally; although others said it was no big deal, it made me feel ineffective compared to other actors. Every acting partner I had intimidated me; they were fluent speakers and therefore more competent and more talented. Amber was frustrated with me because she said on many occasions that I could be working and booking roles if I put myself out there. But I wasn't willing to do that, not even for her.

Fan Expo. Kid. Candy store. Rory, Paul and I were at Vancouver's version of Comic-Con in San Diego: a geek's paradise with comics, toys, cosplay and science fiction actors signing autographs and having photos taken. I didn't know where to look or go first— Ireland had nothing like this. The people walking around were dressed as their favourite characters: Superman, Spiderman and more obscure comic and video game characters. Phasers, tricorders and sonic screwdrivers were on display; there was even a TARDIS from *Doctor Who*.

Rory and I lost Paul to the comic book section the instant we walked into the Expo, and then Rory walked off to find some food. I was engrossed in the new Generation 1 Transformer figures when my phone buzzed. I looked at the message from Rory: Amanda Tapping is signing photos over here.

I went weak at the knees. Amanda Tapping, the "Queen of Science Fiction" was here! At the actor autograph area, the line to meet her was massive. I sauntered into the back of the line and Paul and Rory joined me, both drinking some kind of fruit smoothies.

"Are you okay?" Rory asked.

"Yeah," I said.

"This is Amanda Tapping, the woman you have been going on about for years. What are you going to say to her?"

"I don't know. Maybe hello."

"Just don't lose your shit," Paul warned. "Professional actors hate that kind of thing."

I had no intention of losing it with her. I was feeling quite calm about the whole thing. It took about forty minutes to get to the front of the line and both Paul and Rory stopped by over that time to check in with me. As I got near to her, I could feel my heart begin to pump faster. I had nothing for her to sign. I saw fans with headshot photos, flags and *SG-1* props for her to inscribe. Crap, am I doing this wrong?

I wasn't going to be crass and ask her to sign my body or anything like that. Paul was right: professional actors hate that kind of thing and I was an actor. I could act calm and collected. Amanda Tapping was, after all, only a person.

By the time I got to the front of the line, I was sweating but determined. I walked up to her and just said, "Thank you."

She looked perplexed. I told her that I had been inspired by her and all the sci-fi shows shot in British Columbia to come to Vancouver and go to acting school.

"Do you have an agent?" the Queen asked.

"No, I am waiting on my permanent residency application before I start looking, but I am still training."

"Stay positive and keep training."

Wanting to be more than a crazed fan, I asked her a question. "As an actor, were you happy with how Samantha's love life evolved?"

This was a valid question. Amanda had played the role of Sam for over ten years and the character had evolved in many ways, as a leader and scientist, but her love life was somewhat disastrous.

"I was happy with it," she said, "but the decisions were not just mine to make."

Sensing my time was up, I asked about where the photos could be taken. All the actors here were earning a fortune on signed head-shots and photos with fans. I knew it was a rather sad, geeky thing to do but I wanted a photo with her, a quality one, not just a selfie in my cell phone. Getting my photo taken with Amanda involved another line-up, $80 and a rather rushed photo session: walk in, get close to famous person, bang, photo taken. The cynics would say this is nothing more than a money-making racket, but the late, great Carrie Fisher put it best in her book, *The Princess Diarist*—she referred to these sessions as lap dances, in which actors break the divide between the screen and the fans, and that does seem uncomfortable. Is it worth $80 a photo? It was to me, and after lining up for thirty minutes, I was greeted by the woman herself.

"Hey, Irish, come over here," Amanda said. We stood side by side, and I was grinning like a fool and blushing. Before I knew it, the photo was taken. No! I wasn't ready! I wanted this photo to be perfect, with me looking cool and confident with the star, a photo I could show my grandchildren with pride. I could have been a diva and made a scene, insisting that the photo be taken again but then I would be one of those crazed fans. I chose to let it go and to accept that whatever photo I got would be the photo I got. I thanked Amanda and the next person, in full *SG-1* army attire, was herded into the booth.

I was crushed. This photo was going to suck and it cost $80! That was the price of a new video game or a steak dinner. I joined yet another line to wait at the developing machine. I can always throw it in the trash if it is horrendous. There I was, beetroot red and my face contorted into a huge grin. Amanda looked amazing, naturally. I looked again at the photo and saw me: not actor Rob, just Rob. I began to laugh and showed the souvenir to Rory and Paul. They laughed too, but I didn't feel hurt at this because, while this wasn't the photo I wanted, it was the photo I needed. I had spent so many years hiding and acting and here now was probably the most authentic photo I had of myself. I had spoken about meeting Amanda in my McGuire support meetings, to people back home and to friends in Vancouver. Now I had. I had done it.

We left the Expo at around 4:00 pm. Rory had to go home as he had evening plans and Paul and I grabbed a coffee.

"This has been the best day ever," I told Paul. "This is why I came here and I feel complete with it."

"So, you're not going to act anymore?" Paul asked. "I really don't know."

I told him about the class I was taking with Amber, and that I enjoyed it, but really deep down didn't know anymore. I was stuck and knew I would have to give up things to move on. I mentioned the book I was working on and Paul was supportive. This day had given me hope. Hope that I could change and that new opportunities would open up, with or without the acting.

Amanda Tapping, the Queen of science fiction, and the geek

19

Dr. Ed and the slow cooker

The week after meeting Amanda Tapping I was still on cloud nine and shared about meeting her at my acting class the following Monday. Was I going to be a professional actor? Maybe and maybe not. It didn't matter. I got home from class at my usual time of around 11:00 pm to find an email reminder in my inbox; it was from Adam and I was due to have my final survey session with him the following week. It had been a whole year! As we arranged our last session for the Friday, part of me was excited while another part was indifferent. Adam had been my "teenage" crush at thirty-three, a step in my sexual development that I couldn't skip. While the idea of being with him was still intoxicating, it wasn't anything more than that. An idea, a dream, like the acting.

Friday came and I arrived at Adam's office. I completed the survey rather quickly as I was single and sexually inactive. I handed it back to him and lingered in his office. There was something I had wanted to ask him all year and with my Amanda Tapping meeting still fresh, I was feeling brave.

"Thanks for everything and if you ever want to grab a coffee, you have my number . . ."

Adam smiled and said, "Thank you, but I have a partner and he may not approve."

"No problem, just thought I should ask," I said as my poor little heart broke.

Adam handled the situation so well, never made me feel weird for asking and I envied his partner even more. As embarrassed as I was, I was proud of myself for asking. Now I knew he was off the market, it allowed me to let him go. The pain eventually gave way to relief but the idea of Adam still lingers and I do use him as a barometer. Every new guy I meet is measured against my Adam scale, on which ginger men automatically get an extra point.

Two months after the loss of Adam I received a call from Jenny. Mum had been hinting over our Skype calls that Nana Iremonger was getting worse. Jenny told me that Nana was not fully conscious and that we all had to come home quickly. The reality of her dying hit me hard; I was at work at the time and began to cry. My boss was sympathetic but no one here could help me, so I dried my eyes and went back into the classroom and finished my day. I would need the money to fly home and I wouldn't get paid for the time I was going to miss. I eventually got back to Tyr's house, booked my flight for the following day and told him that I was flying home immediately. I was calmer than I thought I would be.

I wanted to see Nana one more time, even if she wasn't conscious, but was prepared to not get that chance. On the flight home I got up to use the washroom, looked out at the rising sun with the clouds beneath it and knew Nana had died.

Arriving in Dublin early in the morning I got the coach home. I got off at Donnybrook and walked the fifteen minutes with my suitcase to Ranelagh village and finally home to Park Drive. It was mid-June 2013 and the weather was unusually warm and sunny. Two large signs with "Sold" in bold red lettering framed the driveway. My parents had been trying to sell the house for years and now finally it was gone too. Another loss.

I went into the house, which was empty, had a shower and changed my clothes. I was walking toward the kitchen when I saw Mum's car come up the driveway. Susan and Mum got out of the car and I opened the door.

"Nana passed away last night," Mum said.

While I had been flying home. I was sad but relieved: Nana was at peace. What worried me more was how Mum would struggle to fill the new void in her life. I cried in private for my lost grandmother, and my lost childhood. Nana Iremonger's parting gift to me was a week home, a week that turned out to be a joyful one.

This was our final chance to spend time in our family home before leaving it forever. I got to spend time with relatives and cousins I hadn't seen in years. Nana's wake and funeral were beautiful and brought us all together. I insisted on speaking at the funeral. I hadn't spoken at Granddad's funeral when he died and I felt I owed them both a few words. I spoke of love and legacy and living every day like it is our last. My suicide attempt was at the forefront of my mind and I felt slightly hypocritical saying that; but then, I was still here and I did have a chance to really live.

I posted about my loss on Facebook because I had had to leave Vancouver suddenly. To my surprise, Rudy sent me a message. We hadn't spoken in months, as he had requested I keep my distance. Hearing from him helped.

I felt stronger and recharged returning to Canada. Over the week, I had spoken about missing my car in Vancouver and many people had said I should take action and get my license. At the time, Irish citizens had to go through the written and practical parts of the driving test before exchanging their licenses in BC. The day after I got back I booked ten driving lessons and took the written portion of the test, which I passed.

The practical test was scheduled for mid-July; despite speeding down an alley and nearly cutting off a bus, I passed that test too. I was thrilled to have my full Canadian license because, like the Xbox, this was a clear commitment to start taking action and control of my life. Then, in late August, I got my permanent residency.

Tyr and I drove to the border and my paperwork was completed. I still had to wait for my actual permanent residency card, which would take a few more months, but I was finally legal in Canada. No more worries about visas or job sponsorship. I was a free agent.

Having all this happen made me feel suddenly terrified. I hated my job but had become comfortable there. I hated my life but had become comfortable with the struggling. It was so familiar. The idea of changing jobs and driving and earning more money and having more freedom paralyzed me. I knew I was the only one who could make these changes and yet I was still stuck, sabotaging myself just as I was about to succeed. How often had I done that before?

Tyr saw this pattern and took it upon himself to begin coaching me. I liked and respected Tyr and he had given me a roof over my head with cheap rent. With his strength, I had always regarded him as powerful. However, I didn't trust him fully. His motives in coaching me and expecting me to share deep secrets just didn't feel right. We danced around this issue for a number of months and it caused tension in the house.

Rudy and I, having reconnected, communicated every few weeks. He was now living in Regina, and I was cautious, not certain about how I felt about us talking again. Rudy was alone for Christmas and, since I was short on money, I promised him I would fly out to Regina rather than home to Dublin for the holidays. The plan was to save money but flying anywhere in December is not cheap. The flight was only a few hours and I arrived in Regina at the stroke of midnight on Christmas Day. On the drive back to his place, Rudy told me he was seeing someone there and another little piece of my heart ached. Part of me thought we might get back together, but now I knew it was off the cards. It was Adam all over again.

"Is your boyfriend all right with me being here?" I asked.

I knew I would not want my boyfriend's ex to stay with him for Christmas.

"Yes, he is okay with this. I told him we are just friends and he is spending the holidays with his family anyway."

I didn't buy his answer fully but, as I was only going to be in Regina for a few days, I decided to enjoy the time we had together. We both Skyped home the following day and, although I missed Ireland, I was grateful to be with Rudy and just veg out and watch lots of *Doctor Who* episodes. It was the first Christmas I really got to relax and rest rather than running around like a mad thing and nothing happened between us either. I slept on the coach, as I respected Rudy too much to damage his new relationship. We agreed to be friends and it was that simple. He cooked and I ate and we hung out. It was a great few days.

I arrived back in Vancouver on December 30, and as the new year was rung in, I could feel a storm coming. Tyr and I continued to lock horns; he pushed me to talk and I got defensive. Living in the same house made it impossible to escape. I gave my month's notice at the beginning of February and that led to a month of the silent treatment. It was a horrible situation; although I understood Tyr was hurt, it felt cruel and justified my decision to stay guarded with him.

This meant another house search. I wanted somewhere closer to the Skytrain network as I was done wasting forty minutes on a bus to get downtown. I viewed various rooms ranging from good to grotty, wanting to be free from Tyr's constant presence. I viewed a room in the Commercial/Broadway area and liked the guy I would be living with. James had worked in the film industry and with Amanda Tapping herself. His place was okay, old and slightly run down, but the room looked good. He did have a cat but I assumed it was like other cats in that it would do its own thing and leave me alone. Tyr had two cats and I hardly knew they were there.

A week later, James offered me the room and Rory helped me move yet again. Living with James was the loneliest experience I have ever had with a roommate. Even basic conversation was a challenge. He was a vegan and plant lover and let the cat run wild. I had agreed to a bi-monthly chore list and after only the second week I was resentful. I had to clean the kitchen, which I never used as the cat was into all the food, along with the shared spaces in the house like the hall and bathroom, all of which were covered with cat hair. James fed this thing on a diet of tuna and yams and it was always starving. You would need five arms and eyes on the back of your head to keep it away when cooking. My solution was to buy a slow cooker and cook with the lid on the pot, but even that wasn't cat proof.

I decided to go home that summer for the cheaper airfare and less hectic schedule. Mum and Dad were renting a small apartment in Rathfarnham after selling our home in Ranelagh and they were renovating a new house five minutes away on Butterfield Avenue. The mere thought of Vancouver and that bloody cat filled me with rage. I was still teaching in the same job, attending acting class, feeling trapped again, and not just with James and the cat. I hated the idea of having to seek professional help but how I was living wasn't working. I wanted a gay counsellor, someone I could relate to and who could relate to me. That would mean having to sacrifice the acting classes. They were not cheap and I wasn't getting the answers I needed from them. My constant fear of stuttering was blocking any kind of talent I might have.

Finding a counsellor was easy. I Googled "gay counsellors in Vancouver" and the first hit I got was Dr. Ed. I sent him an email enquiring about his services. Most professionals in Vancouver have a free twenty-minute introduction session to see if counsellor and patient can work together.

"Where would you like to start?" Dr. Ed asked.

"At the beginning," I said.

He then asked me if I had any questions.

"Do you want to love me, save me or have sex with me?" After everything I had been through over the last few years I didn't trust anyone, especially men claiming to be able to help me.

After a brief pause, Dr. Ed said, "No."

I trusted him. He was gay and professional and went to the same gym as me. I had recognized him the instant I walked into his office. I was ready to talk and to listen to him. I was ready to move beyond stuttering, being gay and suicide attempts. I was ready to look past being a victim and, more than anything, I wanted to change. A life away from cats and teaching. I wanted to become the man Nana Iremonger knew I could be and I wanted to save the Beast, still waiting in the hangar, out of sight but never out of mind.

Paying someone to listen to me was a huge support. This was a professional and confidential relationship. The initial sessions were intense, to say the least. I didn't realize how angry I was. Angry with people and myself.

We focused on the early childhood bullying and my stuttering and I remember losing it in fits of rage. The pain that was there below the rage was hard to live with. All these toxic, hateful emotions began to spill from me like emotional vomit. I felt exhausted after each session and sad because I still couldn't forgive myself for it all. I blamed my six-year-old self for letting this happen. I also blamed Mum and Dad. They had failed me, I believed, because they had subscribed to what my idiot teachers had told them about me being a victim and weak. Was it any wonder I was a broken, empty shell of a man? The stuttering was an extension of all that pain. I was terrified to open my mouth, I was terrified to be seen, I was terrified to be loved. I was always terrified. Dr. Ed took me back to the early stuttering occurrences, like the music class when I couldn't say tuba or trombone. More than twenty years after that trauma, I couldn't say those words as I sat on his couch. I remember wailing, "Please stop this. I can't, I can't go there."

For the Beast and for my future, I knew I would have to and I resented it. This therapy was another form of torture and I was paying him for it! We spent about six months going through it all and by December we were beginning to move beyond my past. I wasn't going home for Christmas that year, as I had been home in June, and I decided to volunteer at a local church to give out food to homeless people on Christmas Day. James didn't celebrate Christmas, but I bought him a few token gifts and some food for the cat. I also bought Dr. Ed a small gift. These were the closest people in my life. Rory was away for the holidays and we did touch base over the season but it was rather low-key.

Volunteering at the church was a new experience and opened my eyes to real suffering and hopelessness. I had suffered, I had felt despair but these poor souls had lived lives I couldn't imagine. I had always had a fear of being a failure and living on the street but being confronted by the reality of it was humbling. I wanted to hide in the kitchen and wash the dishes but was sent to serve coffee, tea and cookies. I was afraid I would stutter on "tea" or "coffee" but I was here for these people. I won't pretend to know what had happened to them, whether it was addiction, family rejection, or just bad luck that had them on the street, many of them starving, but being able to give them a meal or a cookie or just a smile made me very grateful for the family I had at home in Ireland, celebrating without me. I was also grateful for my ability to cope in Vancouver and pay my bills and now afford counselling.

I was grateful for the Beast sitting in the hangar, I was grateful to Rory for being there and to Rudy who was celebrating this Christmas with his family. This realization was my gift that year.

I went home, made a pizza and recalled that day in the hangar, two years before. I wasn't going to let fear stop me. I wasn't going to give up on myself.

The most painful lesson I had learned through counselling was that I was afraid to want things. Sure, I said I wanted more money but could I accept that? No. I said I wanted love and I described the fantasy that was Adam but, if he turned up on my doorstep professing his love, could I accept that? No. I hated my job and said I wanted to change, but did I? No. I could say it was fear but it wasn't. I could say it was confusion, that I didn't know what to do and that was another lie. The real source of my fear was myself. I truly believed I was a broken, stuttering homosexual. A worthless person who would always struggle. I tried to be fixed, I had tried to run, I had tried to end it all and, as I sat there with my pizza, I could see that I feared not being broken. Who would that version of me be and could I step into that?

2015 began quietly. I was back working and back in counselling. I returned to Dublin in February as Jenny was visiting with my new niece, Sophie, who was six months old and being christened in Ireland. Mum and Dad were in their new home, which felt like a new family home with all of us there, and having a baby in the house really lit my parents up.

Two weeks later, I was back in Vancouver and I could hear the cat's patter of paws the instant I put my key in the door. I wanted to cry. I had spoken to Dr. Ed about my living arrangements, saying I was fine for now. I wasn't. The cat gave me fleas a few weeks later after James accusing me of bringing home bed bugs. He also began dating a girl with a dog and it was like a trauma flashback to Rory and Tegan. The first time I heard them having sex, I was done and on the internet. Ten minutes later, I found a one-bedroom suite three minutes away. I viewed it and put down a deposit immediately. I told James I was leaving and paid a full month's rent in lieu of notice. I didn't care about the money, I just wanted out of that house. I was proud of myself: I'd taken action, I was free and I'd made a positive change in my life.

20

Finding love on the back of a trailer

I met Sachi at the Vancouver Acting School and we were friendly but not as close as I would have liked; she had depth and power and I called her my dark horse. Every few weeks we'd have coffee and share our news. Sachi knew I had stopped acting class to pay for my counselling and that I'd recently moved. She was pleased for me and excited for herself, telling me about the self-development course she'd recently completed. The Cornerstone conference had given her the tools to change her life, she explained. I was sceptical. How many courses promise that? For my part, I was more than happy with talking to Dr. Ed. Sachi said it would change my life, and for her sake I went along to see what it was all about.

The introduction session was full of happy, smiling people. It struck me as a cult and I decided not to sign up. Three months later, Sachi invited me to another session for the latest course she had done. I didn't want to be difficult and said yes. It was the same marketing pitch. I said no again, claiming money issues. But I did notice a change in Sachi. She seemed happier, lighter and she had booked three acting roles, including one lead. Two months later, she asked me to a home introduction session, which was again aimed at getting me to sign up. I was annoyed and felt cornered but a little curious.

"If I sign up for this thing will you stop asking me to these sessions?"

"Yes, I will," she promised.

I signed up and paid my deposit. I was enrolled into the next Cornerstone course on June 19 and found myself in a large room with about one hundred and twenty people all sitting in quiet anticipation. It was a lot like the McGuire Programme and I felt like I was betraying them in some way by being there.

On Friday, the first day, I sat in the back of the room, observed what was happening and sulked. The course leader was talking about how we lived our lives through story and I was very attached to my story. Hell, I was writing a book about it. I was the broken stuttering homosexual with a race car. I listened to other people, some of whom had far worse traumas than mine to share and were coached by the leader. I could see people getting lighter as they shared. The day was long and we finished at 10:00 pm.

As I walked home I was in turmoil. My story had shaped my life. It was the reason I suffered and apparently it was all my own doing. I didn't want to share or be exposed and I certainly didn't want to take responsibility for all that had happened to me as a child. I asked myself the same terrifying question I had asked after my first McGuire Programme: who would I be without my stutter?

The next day, Saturday, was more of the same. An early start and back on our chairs for 9:00 am. I sat closer to the front of the room this time and the topic of conversation shifted away from us and our story to how our behaviour affected others. This was not going to be pleasant. As I listened to people sharing, I got the very clear understanding that I wasn't a nice person to be around. That Mum, Dad, Jenny and Susan had been walking on eggshells around me for years. My stutter, my acne, my homosexuality. I must have been very challenging, a ticking time bomb of angst and rage. But that was not the worst of it. Love came up next. How people around us tried to love us and we couldn't see it for what it was.

I knew I recoiled from love. It made me feel uncomfortable. I felt I didn't deserve to be loved, so saw it as fake whenever someone told me they loved me.

As the course leader talked, I fixated on Dad. I thought my father and I had a great relationship and that he had never done me wrong, but what I was getting as I sat there on my chair was that I had something going on about him. I had assumed he was ashamed of me as a child after the bullying and the stuttering therapy. I had assumed he saw me as weak with the acne and running from my job. I had assumed he was disappointed that I was gay. Having to take responsibility for these assumptions was something I had never done before. I blamed the world and I played the victim very well. I thought about the cars I had owned. Dad had helped me buy 729-UZO. He had spent weeks working on 88-MO-2911, cleaning it and sourcing all the GTI trim. He had done that for me. He has been keeping 98-D-1333 maintained at home for me rather than just selling it.

I'm a selfish asshole.

Then I remembered the Beast. I could feel tears of shame streaming down my cheeks. Dad had kept the Beast just as he had promised nearly twenty years ago. He took it out of storage to get me driving it and I resented him for pushing me. I resented the Beast itself for being so conspicuous; I was mad at them both. I resented Dad for never saying he loved me in words. It is an Irish thing: both he and Nana O'Brien use phrases like "Now take care of yourself," rather than saying those three simple words I wanted and needed to hear from him. Yet, looking at his actions, remembering a slightly dusty M3 on a trailer being hauled up to be serviced and reconditioned, I finally understood that was him expressing his love for me.

For thirty minutes before our break, I cried, remembering the Beast sitting on the trailer. It was a perfect expression of love and

I had missed it. How many other signs had I missed? I had been blind to it and my poor father, all that effort to reach me while my own stories and thoughts were continuously getting in the way. How many times have I thrown love back in his face?

As the lunch break approached we were given the assignment to be in communication with people. I knew I was phoning Dad straight away. It was 1:00 pm in Vancouver so that meant it was 9:00 pm in Dublin. The break was only thirty minutes and there was a gaggle of people around the building, so I went a little further afield. Vancouver has lovely little hidden park areas; I found a deserted one and sat on a bench. Taking a few deep breathes, I dialled Dad's number.

"Rob, is everything okay?"

I could hear mild panic in his voice—he wasn't expecting this call. My usual time to ring him and Mum was on a Sunday using Skype.

"Hi, Dad. No, everything is fine, don't worry." Before I lost my nerve, I continued. "I'm doing this self-development course called Cornerstone and I really wanted to talk to you." I was embarrassed, because Dad felt I was always doing courses and this was just another one on a long list.

"I've been sitting on a chair for over a day now and I realize that I have been an asshole to you. I was blaming you for my life and making you wrong for not saying you loved me." This was Cornerstone-speak to a certain extent so I tried to make it clear. "I thought you were ashamed of me and I resented you for it. I thought you saw me as weak and I hated you for that. Now I see it was all me, it was all in my head."

I was on a roll. "You kept the M3 and put in on a trailer to be serviced for me and I am sorry that I totally missed the sentiment. You take care of my car and I never say thank you. When I decided to come to Vancouver to be an actor you never questioned it. God, when I came out as gay, you were thrilled." I was crying. "I am so sorry and I love you and I promise you that I will not play the victim anymore."

There was silence on the other end of the phone for a few seconds. "Rob, I've been telling you that for years." He was laughing. That was not what I expected. "I know what the cars mean to you and I have never been ashamed of you. I've worried and been saddened by your struggle with life but never ashamed."

I was speechless and I felt so much lighter. I wanted more time but was due to go back to the room and I still had to grab some food.

"Thanks, Dad. I will talk to you soon, and I l-l-love you."

I bought a banana and shoved it into my mouth. It would have to be enough until dinner. I was still weepy in the room and knew I had to get up to the microphone. I put my hand up and walked up to the microphone at the front of the room. There was a speaker in front of me so I got to linger there, wondering what I was going to say. I wasn't afraid to talk, to share, and, when my turn came, it all came flooding out.

"I'm Rob, and I want to apologize to the room. I have been sitting on my chair for the last day fighting this process and sulking. I had it that I was a broken stuttering homosexual who attempted and failed to commit suicide and I have been so attached to my story that I wrote it down as a manuscript and gave it to my family. Eh, I got today that my Dad loves me through the memory of a car, a special car actually, and I phoned him on the break. I just want to say thank you. Thank you so much. He was not mad at me or ashamed and I see that he loves me and I feel so much lighter."

The room was silent and then the leader spoke up. "What did you get from the call?" he asked.

"I got love. I got my father back, even though I had never lost him but I felt I had. For years, I felt I had."

"Are you a broken stuttering homosexual?" was the next question.

"I don't know. I usually stutter when I am nervous but right now I see possibilities for the future."

"That was powerful, thank you, and I hope you speak up more over the next two days." I was applauded and went to sit down.

I shared over the weekend and phoned Mum later that day.

"I love you for helping me keep the Beast and always having my back. Oh, and is Dad okay?"

"He was very emotional after your call," Mum told me.

I phoned Sachi in tears and thanked her from the bottom of my heart. I told her everything I had done and said, and asked her to the final session on Sunday night.

By Sunday, we were getting to the end of the course. We still had the graduation session on Tuesday but the last session on Sunday night was special for me. It was an opportunity to invite the person who had enrolled you in the course. For me that was Sachi. She arrived late because her life was now busy and successful. She had been at an audition and when she arrived I jumped up.

"This amazing and beautiful woman has saved my life. The things I have done this weekend, the person I can see myself becoming . . . God, thank you." Looking at Sachi directly, I said, "I never really understood what friendship was before this. I hated you for pushing me over and over again into this work and now I see why you did it. You love me and care for me." Sachi was in tears and I was in tears. I went over to her and we hugged and sat there together until the end of the night. I had never felt closer to a person and was so grateful for that. I immediately signed up for the next, more advanced course three months away and was excited about it.

That night I lay awake open to the possibilities of my life and I saw so much love. I could see my toxic story for what it was and the Beast sitting on the trailer now felt very different. It represented the future and I was going to create that. Not for it or me, but for us, and for the simple reason that I saw now that I could do it.

21

Optimus Robert: The Transformer

I admit to becoming a bit of a Cornerstone junkie from that point on. I had operated in a space of fixing myself while still relating to my story as a broken stuttering homosexual and it hadn't worked. I was running from the idea that I wasn't really broken in the first place. It terrified me.

What would my life be like if I could just accept it and move on rather than being stuck in this never-ending cycle? What if I was fine with being gay and owning my own sexuality. What if I could be my authentic, powerful self in a professional setting, be it acting or anything else. These were my thoughts but to get there would require changing everything I thought I knew about myself.

The first thing I saw was that I had no idea how to relate to people, either friends or lovers. Sachi had shown me what true friendship was and I was uncomfortable feeling that bond. At the first conference, I sat beside a woman called Amy and we bonded over our shared uncertainty of what was coming next. She saw me break down and cry on the Saturday, she heard me talk throughout the weekend, and I supported her too. After it was all done, I walked out, assuming I would never to see or hear from her again.

Amy would phone me on a weekly basis after the course and I couldn't understand why she was doing that. I hated talking on the phone and felt stressed because I wasn't sure what to say. What does she want from me? This went on for weeks and I had to tell someone so I asked Rory. Was Amy some stalker freak who was latching on to me? I wasn't going to let that happen. I told Rory all this, exasperated.

"And I'm bloody gay so I will never fuck her." Rory laughed in my face.

"Maybe she wants to be your friend."

"Why? I don't want to be my friend."

"Well, Rob, I think that is why she is phoning you. She knows you are gay and you went through this course together and maybe that is it." He was right. I asked Amy on our next call and she laughed too. She knew I was gay and was very happy being single. She has been a rock for me ever since, because transformation is not easy.

Susan repeatedly invited me down to visit her in California and I finally took her up on the offer, much to her surprise. I may not have had a lot of money and I was busy, but I was sick of saying that. It was a short flight and she was putting me up so the trip wouldn't leave me too tight for money. I told her all about the work I was doing with Cornerstone and she was supportive.

That weekend we did the Warner Brothers Studio Tour, which began on the Ellen show set followed by the sets where Pretty Little Liars was shot. I felt the old acting buzz and explained how sets work to Susan. It was great to have all this knowledge but, never having proven my mettle, I felt like a bit of a fraud too.

We ate candy and cupcakes for lunch and arrived at what was pitched as the high point of the tour, a re-creation of the Central Perk coffee shop from the sitcom *Friends*. I was so excited to be there I wasn't really paying attention to what this part of the tour included. There was to be an interactive taping of a scene, filming people on the set as one of the characters, to be superimposed into the *Friends* episode—video-editing magic, basically.

They were looking for volunteers and I said, "I'll do it. Who am I going to be?"

"Joey."

I was more like Ross or Chandler, but those roles were already filled. So I sat on the sofa in the middle of the set with the other volunteers as everyone else looked on. The tour guide played the original clip and I suddenly realized what was going to happen. We were going to have to reenact the scene. Oh, shit. I wanted to bolt up from the sofa and run but there was the tour guide, the tourists and Susan. Where can I run to? The clip finished, the cameras turned to us. My mouth was dry and I tried to concentrate and breathe. I could see my lines being fed to me just out of the frame and I was a trained actor. I began to read from the cue card.

"Th-Th-Th mmmmm Thursday, th-tha-that is H-H-H-Hallo, Halloween."

I stuttered my way through the line. I could feel everyone's eyes on me and I couldn't look at Susan. I felt so exposed and embarrassed.

After the scene ended, we got up and I went over to Susan. "That could have gone better," I said, trying to laugh it off.

"Don't worry about it," Susan said. "At least you stood up and did it."

In the past, I would have lost it and been furious, crying and screaming. This bloody stutter really was ruining my life. For Susan's sake, I tried to put on a brave face and we went on with the tour. I was trying very hard just to accept that it hadn't been great. I wouldn't see any of these people again and it really didn't matter, except to me. It wasn't perfect, I wasn't perfect. All my old feelings of being broken were right there in my space. I had learned enough so far to see that I had a choice to make. I could choose to make myself wrong or I could choose to just accept it and move on. At the end of the tour Susan and I made our way to the car.

"So how bad was I on the *Friends* set, really?" I asked.

"I think it was worse for you than for us but I am sorry regardless. It can't have been easy for you."

I was sitting on my anger and disappointment. Letting it go was a real challenge. This was why I wasn't acting. It's why I hadn't changed jobs and it was why I was still single. It went beyond the speech dysfluency; this was the story of my life.

"Look, I really admire your courage for volunteering and doing it. I wouldn't have," Susan continued.

I appreciated what she said but courage was not the issue. I knew I didn't lack courage but I lacked something else and that was space to explore. I returned to Vancouver the next night feeling refreshed. I unpacked my backpack and carefully gathered my passport and permanent residency card and put them with my laser card and credit card in a small bag in my bedroom dresser. I normally hide them in a better place, but it was late and I was tired. Monday came and went and Tuesday was a Cornerstone seminar night so I left everything where it was. Coming home late, I was greeted by a gash on my door. *Now what?*

I opened the door and held my breath, expecting to find my place either ransacked or bare. It was neither and that added to my confusion.

What the hell is going on?

My TV and video game consoles were still there and everything seemed accounted for. My desk had been messed up and I noticed things on the ground. I went into my room and found my laptop under my pillow. I breathed a sigh of relief. It was a new MacBook Pro and if it had been stolen I had no idea what I would do. I sat on the edge of the bed and noticed my dresser drawer was open.

Oh, bollocks!

Looking in the drawer, I saw my passport, PR card, license and Irish bank cards had been stolen. This theft was specific, and now I had no paperwork. I had no way to get home or to re-enter

Canada and I had no proof of identity proof except for my soon-to-expire Canadian driver's license.

I knocked on my landlord's door, praying that David, his English speaking son would be home. Panic made me stutter all over the place. I was nearly in tears as I explained, "I have no paperwork, no passport or PR card. This is serious. Do you or I phone the police?" As the tenant, it was my responsibility to make the call and making it transported back to the couch in Central Perk: my stutter was in full swing and I was barely understandable. I then rang Dad.

"Everything is fine but I have been broken into. My p-p-p-passport has been stolen along with my P-P-PR card and Irish driver's license and bank cards." I could cancel the bank cards but the Irish embassy was thousands of miles away in Ottawa, so I asked Dad to notify the passport office and cancel it from home as it was early morning there.

"Everything will be fine, Rob," Dad said.

Mum came on the line as Dad phoned the passport office and we spoke for a while. I was calmer now and resigned to the fact that this had happened and I was going to have to cope. I let my parents go and I texted my boss, telling him what had happened and that he would need to find a substitute teacher for the next day. I then texted my Cornerstone coach to share with her what had happened, highlighting the fact that I was dealing with the situation.

Did it matter? Well yes and no. I obviously wanted to be fluent and struggled as a result. I know if this had happened a year before, I wouldn't have coped at all. I would have totally shut down and been in a panic. For me, this was a major transformation.

When I shared the break-in with friends, they all asked almost immediately, "When are you moving?"

"I'm not moving."

"But someone must have been watching you and that is serious."
It was, but what could I do about it?

"The way I see it, everything of value has been stolen. They can come back and take everything else for all I care. I am happy where I am living and I am not moving again."

It took a few months to get everything replaced and I now rent a safe deposit box in the bank for all my important documents. I wasn't going to let this happen again.

As all this was happening in the background of my life, Amy and I had worked our way through the Cornerstone curriculum. We were now both doing a five-month course which consisted of planning a community project. I decided to do an LGBTQ speed dating event. Partly because I wanted to raise awareness of queer suicide and partly to find a boyfriend. I had been single and celibate since breaking up with Rudy and this was another area I felt I needed to get a handle on.

The planning stage was easy: I approached a charity in Vancouver that specialized in suicide prevention and they came on board, with the event would raise funds on their behalf. Having to share my own experience of suicide was cathartic too. A venue was booked and the promotion began. I had planned to promote it over a month but the project was two weeks behind schedule so I had less than fourteen days to pull it off. I appeared on a local radio station, had a Facebook promotion with daily countdown videos and even raffled myself off for a jar of candy that no one bid on.

On the night of the event I had about twenty promises on Facebook, not a reliable measure of attendance. I sat in the venue waiting for 7:00 pm, the appointed starting time. I had *EVO*, a car magazine, with me to serve as a distraction from what my gut was asking me. *What if no one comes?* I had to just face the fact that what was going to happen was going to happen—there was nothing I could do but get through the night. I was already mad at the amount of work I had put into this event and the personal cost of sharing my own story to the world on Facebook. You are not a failure, I told myself. Even if no one comes it will be okay, it is only a dating event. No one will die.

I was so busy trying to hold myself together that I nearly missed the first guest arriving followed by Amy, who was there to support me. Being on the same course, I knew she knew what was involved in pulling this off. Nicola, a work friend, also came to support me along with one of my acting friends, Vivian. In total, we had five guests: two men and three women. There was no speed dating that night and we gathered our chairs around in a circle and had a great time chatting about dating and dating disasters. The venue didn't even charge me for the space. Ironically, I collected $300 dollars in donations from people who didn't attend the event. Most were gay men I had dated or met over the years and they wanted to support the cause.

My perception on the whole event changed two weeks later in our next course classroom. I was angry, having had time to stew over the event, telling Amy that I had failed and I was done. "Just relax. Your event happened and you did great. There is nothing to be mad about," she assured me.

"Oh, yeah. I'm sure all five people who came were totally satisfied with their night. Fuck sake. Five people, Amy, FIVE! I worked my ass off for that and now I have to sit through this! No, I am done, Amy. Sod this."

I stood up, grabbed my bag and coat, and walked out. Amy sat there staring at me and I didn't want her to come after me. I was livid and done. As I got out into the cold, my rage abated and I felt embarrassed for my outburst. I am not running from this. I ran whenever things got hard or didn't go my way. After all this work, I wasn't going to run again. I went back into the room and placed my bag and coat down. I apologized to Amy and sat there until the end of the night. I didn't run. I chose to stay. This work was changing me and I wanted to see where it would lead. I wanted it to lead back to the Beast and to me embracing a life I loved.

The next two courses made up the Communication Curriculum, which involved two weekend sessions, a few months apart. Amy wanted to do them, and so I found myself listening to her.

"You could be very powerful with communication," she teased me.

It is only two weekends and then I am done.

The first weekend came in early April and I arrived to find Amy at the front of the room holding a seat for me.

"I can't wait to see what I get out of this weekend," she exclaimed.

"I hope I survive this weekend," I joked.

"You're just still upset over your dating event!"

"Yes, I am."

The instructor was someone new to us, a powerful man called Charlie. He was in his late fifties and had kind eyes but a no-prisoner attitude. As this was an advanced course, we jumped straight in. Powerful communication was the key and, as a stutterer, this was something that I had feared my whole life. The simple act of communication had been a challenge and now having to bring my own power to it did not come easily.

The most striking thing I got from the weekend was from a request exercise. I was handed a sheet with simple requests: take out the trash, could you please close the door. I saw that weekend that I had made my dating project harder than it needed to be because I had done it all myself. I was not accustomed to asking for help and I had declined a few offers of assistance. I was scared to bring other people on board because then I would have had to play big, pick up the phone and share what I was doing. Part of me was still fighting this process. I saw my ability to communicate as compromised. Amy and I made a pact to finish the curriculum by taking the second course in June.

Those two months free of courses were liberating; I cut back on my teaching hours to write and explore the possibility of self-publication. I felt excited and transformed. That was my mindset walking into the second and final communication course. Charlie was leading it again and I loved this guy. Strong, funny and no-nonsense. This two-day course focused on using our new communication skills to create a world around us. I got up and shared about my manuscript.

"So, what is next?" Charlie asked me.

"I'm going home," I said, not mentioning the fact that I wasn't sure if it would be for good or not. This course was a bit of a blur. I heard people talking about what they were going to create and I knew they would succeed, but I had no idea what I was going to create after the manuscript was published. I had a vague idea of making videos and launching a website and Amy, among others, had suggested I become a motivational speaker. I knew I had a choice of doing that in Ireland or Canada.

On Sunday evening, we had the opportunity to sign up for yet another Cornerstone course, a year-long leadership and communication program called Squad. A year. A year of intense training. *Hell, no.* I was going to take another ten-week seminar instead and keep working that way. The time came to sign up and I deliberately left the room. If I was sitting on my chair, I would be an easy target for sure, to be approached by various people looking to enrol and sign me up. I went outside and felt something gnawing in my gut. A familiar feeling. The feeling I felt when I decided to come to Vancouver to act and the feeling I had when I knew it was time to come out.

God, no, please. I don't want to do this. There was some part of me that wanted more. Not more courses but more transformation.

If I went home for good would I really change my world when left to my own devices? I went back into the room and we began our final session. Charlie stood up and congratulated all the people who had signed up. Three people had, including Amy. Amy signed up! I couldn't believe it. At the next break, I walked over to her. "You signed up?"

"Yeah, I followed your example," she said.

"What example? Amy, I didn't sign up."

"But I saw you crying and assumed you'd signed up."

"I always cry at these bloody things. I didn't sign up."

"Well, I'm not doing this alone," she told me.

"You are not doing it alone. It is called Squad for a reason."

"I think you want to sign up."

"I am curious," I confessed, "to see what I could achieve or become in the next year."

"You're signing up with me."

I sat back down in my chair for the final session and, over the two hours, got to make my decision. At the end of the night, I was almost ready to sign up. If there was any doubt in my mind it was about to be expunged. I saw Amy walking towards me with Charlie.

"So, why not Squad?" he asked.

"Look, I am thinking about it but I have no money and I am working part-time now."

"So, why not Squad?" he asked again.

What is it with these people and repeating themselves?

"We can do it together," Amy said, breaking the silence. That was when I began to cry.

"I'm scared to do this," I mumbled. "It is a year and I have no money and I don't want to. I want to go home."

If I signed up I wouldn't be going home for another year. I wouldn't have anywhere to run and hide. I would not be able to fall back into my old ways of being. I wanted more for my life and was tired of the same old struggle but this was going to be work? Amy took my hand and walked me up to the sign-up table. Charlie nodded in approval and went to talk to other people in the room.

I was in full sobbing mode as I signed myself up, pulling out my credit card. *What am I doing?*

As I signed the form, I thought of the Beast in the hangar, waiting for me. I cried some more because that was my answer. I was doing it for us.

I hugged Amy.

"We are going to rock this," she said.

I wasn't so sure, but I was happy to be on this journey with her. As with Sachi, I felt a real, loving connection with her and knew we would be okay because we had each other's back.

I booked a trip home for a holiday in June, when Jenny and her family would be flying over to celebrate my niece's second birthday.

22

Waiting in the wrong pub

I felt a new wave of confidence and ease as I flew home. I had a clear commitment for the next year and I knew I would face massive challenges but was ready to see where they would lead me. No one back home had seen me over the past year, during which I had been through so much already. I hoped I had changed and wanted to prove to myself that I could be more than what I believed.

Seeing Dean and Zara at the airport to pick me up told me I was home. Dean hugged me and I turned to Zara, grabbed her and hugged the life out of her.

"So, have you gotten any pole in Vancouver?" she asked, laughing, when I released her.

"Jesus, Zara, I'm only five minutes off the plane. No. Still single."

It was a valid question. I had been single since breaking up with Rudy; even though I had reconnected with him, I was still solo and celibate. Zara wasn't the only one asking me that question and I had no answer. I was still apprehensive of men and sex. I still felt shame around my attraction to men, especially hairy ginger ones. There was something stopping me from letting go, but I was ready to explore whatever that might be.

The first few days at home were all about watching Sophie and celebrating her second birthday. People asked me how I was doing and I said I was doing well, committed to Squad and Vancouver for the next year. No one knew what I was talking about or what it meant to me. Susan, who arrived home a day after me, was convinced it was a crutch and we had a heated argument about it. I got mad and emotional and told her she wasn't listening to me.

Amy and I had a Skype date planned to book our plane tickets to Minneapolis, our first Squad trip in August, and I was never so grateful to talk to her. She helped me through it. I knew what I was doing was my choice and I didn't have to defend it to Susan or anyone else. As we booked our tickets the internet crashed. I panicked and Amy again calmed me down. I was home but I found myself wanting to be closer to Amy and the new world we were living in together.

"I miss you," I said.

"I miss you, too, but we are going to do this!"

On this trip home, numerous things occurred that would have knocked me out of the game in the past: 98-D-1333 overheating on a trip down the M50 motorway, having to deal with banking issues in my local bank, getting lost trying to find Dean's new rat-infested home on the outskirts of Dublin. Making it all mean nothing brought the freedom to deal with each situation as it arose, and I took responsibility for it all. Cars do overheat, banks can be irritating and I do, on occasion, get lost in the city. There was no drama and nothing wrong with any of it. I was changing and my perception of myself was changing too—for the better. I felt proud.

Back to the dating question. Why was I still single? While I was home and dealing with all these things, I knew there was one person I could connect with and explore this question. I hadn't spoken to Matthew since before my suicide attempt. We had kept connected via Facebook and he had heard about what I had attempted to do when I shared my story on social media to help promote my LGBTQ speed dating event. I felt it was the right thing to at least sit down and have a coffee with him. I rang Matthew on the cell number I had on my Irish phone for him and got no answer. I was relieved and ended up sending him a text. I waited a few days and got no reply. I was very tempted to just leave it at that. The old me would have assumed he didn't want to talk, but I knew better now.

That could have been an old number and you can use Facebook to reach out.

I typed a message to him. *Hi, Matthew, I am home for a week. Can I buy you a beer or a coffee?*

I tried to make it as casual as I could, but those words were emotionally loaded. He responded and we arranged to meet in a local pub in Terenure that Friday. He had moved since and changed phone number too. I stupidly never asked for this new number and he didn't volunteer it.

On the day we were due to meet I hit the local gym. I was nervous to meet Matthew but I was going to be as buff as I could be and I had paid a lot to join this gym for only two weeks. Then I went out with Mum to help her with decorating her new office in the house. We set up a new printer and hung curtains; I was conscious of the time but I knew I was doing all this work to distract myself from my nervousness. At 7:00 pm, I showered and put on the best shirt I had in my suitcase. It felt slightly tight on me.

"Mum, it this shirt okay on me? It feels slightly tight?" I asked.

"It looks fine, just open the top button."

I was due to meet Matthew at 7:30 pm so I took the Polo and drove off. Parking was easy and I found the pub. I ordered myself a beer and waited. 7:30 pm came and went and I began to sweat.

Maybe he is just late.

I didn't have his phone number and he didn't have mine either, having changed my own number. I looked at my watch: 7:45 pm. By 8:00 pm I knew something was wrong. Matthew was a decent guy and I didn't think he would stand me up. I had a horrible sinking feeling in my gut.

God, what if I got it wrong?

I sprinted out of the pub and drove home. It only took ten minutes and I jumped on Facebook and messaged him.

I am so sorry, Matthew, I got the pub wrong. Can I have your mobile number? I typed.

He sent his number and I dialled it immediately without thinking. "Matthew, I am so sorry and I take full responsibility for this mess up. I was nervous to meet you and I didn't check the pub's name properly. If you are still there I can be there in ten minutes."

Mum was in the kitchen with me watching this all unfold. "Cool. I'll be there in ten, and thank you, Matthew."

I nodded at Mum. "I messed up. I'll be home later."

I drove back to the same parking spot and ran into the pub across from the one I had been sitting in to find Matthew in the beer garden. It was getting dark but still warm outside. I greeted him and gingerly hugged him.

"I am so sorry again," I said sheepishly. "Why didn't you check?" he asked. "Like I said, I was nervous."

"Why?" he asked

Fuck sake, why do you think! Part of me thought he was messing with me but I answered anyway. "It had been years since we have spoken and I wanted to talk to you, to give you an opportunity to talk to me. I felt we left things a little unfinished."

Being vulnerable sucks!

He asked me about my suicide attempt. "Why didn't you reach out to me?" he asked.

I told him I couldn't reach out to anyone and that it was a dark place to be in.

"What was going on with you anyway? You were so weird that trip home—talking about your sister's wedding like it was all about you," Matthew said.

I felt sick sitting there but wanted to give him a chance to say or ask whatever he had to. This was the baggage that was holding me back.

"I was lost, Matthew. I had broken up with Rudy. I was lonely, tired and scared. Jenny getting married made me feel like a failure as I am the eldest child and the only son. I wanted it to be me. I wanted to be happy and I wanted to feel something more than despair. It wasn't a gay thing; it was me and the way I saw myself. I felt I had hurt you and was a mess of a boyfriend when we dated. I was using you but not really there and I wanted to say I am sorry if I hurt you."

There, it was out there: how I really felt, and now it was over to him. He paused for a few seconds.

"I knew where you were at when we dated. You didn't hurt me. I wasn't brokenhearted or anything like it. It just didn't work out and that is fine."

I had been waiting to hear those words for years. I got teary-eyed. "Thank you, Matthew. Really. Thank you for saying that."

"Are you okay now?" he asked.

"I am very well. I have a group of very supportive people around me and I have had years to deal with all my issues." Poor Dr. Ed, and Amy, and everyone else close to me.

"Glad to hear it," Matthew replied.

I was thankful he didn't dig any deeper. It was a long story and I really didn't want to recount it to him at that moment.

He can read all about it when the book is published.

We sat for a few more hours and just hung out, very much like old times. It was a carefree night and he had freed me in a way I wasn't even aware of yet. I offered to drop him home and as we got his new place, which was close to my dad's office, we paused.

"Do you want to come in for tea?' he asked.

Part of me wanted to say yes but a bigger part knew I couldn't. I had just mended a fence and we'd agreed to be friends, to keep in touch. Doing anything else now would sully that commitment. As he walked into his house and closed the door, I sat in 98-D-1333 for a few minutes. I was a lucky man to have people like this in my life.

Arriving home at 12:30 am, I could see lights still on in the house. *Mum must be waiting up. Some things will never change.*

I looked at my old companion's worn steering wheel, the torn gear lever gaiter and the small crack above the air vent nearest to me. I've missed you, I thought, patting the Polo's dashboard. This car had seen me through so much. Although the Beast was closest to my heart, this car was a reminder of who I had been for years. I went into the house and walked up quietly to my mother's room, knocking on her door.

She was sitting up, waiting.

"I wasn't expecting you home," she said. "How was it?"

"Intense, initially," I admitted. "After that we just hung out. It was great to see him again."

"Why did you agree to meet him?"

"Some part of me needed to. I needed to clean up with him and this is the kind of man I am choosing to be."

That answer felt right to me.

"I was impressed with how you handled yourself tonight," Mum said. I lunged towards her and gave her a huge hug. I really needed to hear that.

I was proud of myself too and to hear that from Mum helped me to see that signing up to do Squad with Amy was the right thing to do.

"But we need to buy you new clothes because that shirt is too tight on you."

"Thanks for saying that, Mum," I said and went down to make a cup of tea.

The next day was Saturday and, true to her word, Mum took me shopping. We went to the Dundrum Town Centre and had lunch as well. The truth of the matter was I really did need clothes that fit me for Minneapolis and throughout the year. We spent the day shopping and I ended up with two new suits that I could mix and match as needed. I felt even more like a man now than I had at the start of the trip.

Since I was due to fly back to Canada on Wednesday, I arranged to make a quick day trip down to Wexford to visit the Beast on the Monday. I wanted to get some photos for a potential book cover as I had been exploring the possibility of self-publication. But it was just an excuse to go and sit in the M3 for a while. Every time I had travelled home and sought refuge here, I was in turmoil and despair. Never knowing what I was doing and getting more desperate as the years went by. This time I was able to just sit there in quiet contemplation.

Who am I becoming? This was an exciting question to ask. Reconnecting with Matthew had allowed me to see myself as a man for probably the first time in my life. The man I got to choose to be. Not out of fear of bullies, authority figures, parents, stuttering or being gay. I had made a promise to this car and I was going to keep it. It was that simple. I was beginning to see I was powerful and the access to this power was to come in the most ironic and unexpected place.

23

Thank you, J.B. of Minneapolis

I arrived back in Vancouver just in time for Gay Pride week and Amy wanted to see the parade. I wasn't interested in the parade, but went for her. We were both counting down the three weeks or so until our trip to Minneapolis and becoming official Squad members. We went to have beer after the parade (finally) ended and to my delight, Ben, my next-door neighbour, joined us with his boyfriend, Alfredo.

Ben and I had met on a blind date and, after deciding to be friends, he moved in next door to me when my landlords asked if I knew of anyone looking for a new home. He was from the UK and we had tea and love of children's cartoons in common. I counted him as a friend and I felt safe having him next door. Ben thought I was a judgmental prude and I gave him the nickname of "dirty little whore" because he, on occasion, kissed on the first date! This was the first time we had hung out socially; I had talked about him a lot to Amy and she wanted to meet him.

We met in a bar on Commercial Drive and the beer began to flow. Alfredo, Ben's new boyfriend, was literally just off the boat and adorably shy. He was very handsome but self-conscious about his English skills as it wasn't his first language. I was in awe of Ben. *How the hell does he do it?*

Ben had talked to me about getting on dating apps like Grindr and Scruff weeks before I went back to Ireland, but it felt wrong and slutty to me.

"Aren't they just sex apps?" I asked.

"Not all the guys on them are after hookups," said Ben.

"So, why are you still single Rob?" Amy jumped in.

"Yeah, Rob, you should get out there," Ben added.

"I'm not ready." Me, defensive.

"I don't buy that," Amy shot back.

"I don't know what I am looking for," I retorted.

"So that is why you need to get out there." Ben, sternly.

"I don't want to. Men are scary and I am too old. I don't want to take the risk again and I don't need sex in my life and besides, Mr. Perfect can find me. That way I won't be responsible when I hurt him and we break up."

"You are full of crap and you are selling yourself short. Give it up and do something about it," Amy said.

That felt rich coming from a single woman but I knew there was no point in trying to deflect attention away from myself.

"Like what?"

"I don't know but do something."

Poor Alfredo was shifting in his seat and we changed the subject. This wasn't a new issue and, after talking to Matthew, I was finally feeling ready to get back into the dating scene.

A few weeks later, as I was writing away one Saturday night, I could hear Ben and Alfredo laughing away at a movie next door. At first I was annoyed. God's sake, why do I have to listen to this? I was feeling sorry for myself and lonely and I was the only one who could change that.

Deal with the dating thing after you finish the manuscript, I told myself. That got me through an hour of writing. Then I had to call bullshit on it. I had been writing for years and could be writing for many more years to come. What if I never finished? And besides, I wanted to discover who I could be in a relationship with another person. To share and grow and be powerfully me. Ben and Amy had my back, as did many others. I wanted to give myself this gift of exploration. I had accepted being gay without every fully embracing it. Sex and my own sexual identity were totally missing in my life; to be authentically powerful and complete as a person, I needed this and I deserved it. No one else would ever give it to me and I wasn't getting any younger.

That night, I signed up to Scruff, the gay dating app, using a cool picture from the Fan Expo with me standing inside a TARDIS. Lacking a ripped body or nude pictures, I knew I would have to use wit and charm in my profile to get any kind of response. I wasn't taking this at all seriously and it was going to be all about having fun.

Reading the profiles, I skipped over the very brief ones and groaned at the overly long ones. I wanted to hit the sweet spot with a profile of just the right length to be enticing. There were strange new terms to learn about too—NSA (no strings attached) sex, and what was this "woofing" thing, the app's digital wolf whistle? Fun being the name of the game, I wrote about *Star Trek* and the *Enterprise* (NCC-1701) exceeding warp 14 and asking where Optimus Prime's trailer disappears to when he transforms. When it came to what I was looking for, I was totally transparent: I didn't want a boyfriend or a relationship, I wrote I was looking for safe, respectful fun. I pressed the upload button and put my phone down. Before I could finish straining my teabag, my phone buzzed. Ben sent me a message.

You are on Scruff! I am thrilled!

I am taking your advice! I typed. *Let's see what happens, hey?*

Good luck! Let me know if I can help in any way.

I put the phone down and went to bed. The next morning, feeling like Jack after the beanstalk had grown in his garden, I had dozens of woofs and messages from a lot of men. I even got my first dick pic and video. I guess they like my profile. I didn't get too excited as I knew I was fresh meat and the first few days you get a lot of attention. Still, I was flattered. Handsome men were messaging me or calling me "sexy" and "handsome." I won't lie— my ego enjoyed it.

I was nervous about the trip to Minneapolis, now less than a week away, and this was a wonderful way to distract myself in a very new and productive way. I got chatting and flirting with a number of guys. One guy, Cheeky Chappy, lived close by and we got flirty quite quickly via text messages. This felt safe to me as it was only texting. I was having fun with it and getting raunchy text messages at work had the days flying by.

A few nights before my trip, I was asked to send my Squad teammates a photo to use on our WhatsApp group. At the same time, Cheeky Chappy wanted a ruder picture of a certain part of my body. I had never taken a dick pic before but I figured, if this was how guys play the game, then I would need a few. I was busy working on my laptop sending both images and for an instant my heart stopped. *Which picture have I sent to who?*

I checked and rechecked about five times.

What if I had sent a dick pic to Squad! I'd be not only mortified but also asked to leave before I'd begun. I texted Cheeky Chappy to confirm which image he had received and he responded that he had received the right image in all its glory, finding the whole near-miss disaster hilarious. This made me feel edgy and powerful; I had just sent my first dick pic, something I never thought I would do. The old me would have said it was wrong and crass but this was the new me, the me who was willing to explore the possibilities of having fun being a gay man. I was also gaining a real appreciation for men in general. Some guys sent messages, others pictures, others woofed. Some wanted sex, others relationships. It was all fine and there was so much choice. It was liberating.

By the second night, I was overwhelmed with the whole thing. The woofs kept coming and I messaged Ben next door.

Can I pop in for a quick chat?

Sure, came the response.

I knocked on Ben's door and he saw the look on my face. "Are you okay?" he asked

"No. It won't stop." I said walking in and putting my phone on his table. Every few minutes it vibrated.

"What do I do?" I asked him. "Do I answer all these guys? Some aren't even in Vancouver."

"No," he said. "Just the ones you like." I felt instantly better.

"You should be flattered," Ben said.

"I am, but I have no idea what I am doing."

"None of us do. Just have fun with it, play as best you can and always feel free to knock on my door."

I hugged Ben and I needed that hug. He was there guiding me, and I needed his guidance.

I kept Scruff on as Amy and I flew into Minneapolis. There was a roaming option and I wanted to see what the good old US of A had to offer. It also helped stem the fear that was rising as we got closer to the hotel. We had to be at the hotel by 4:00 pm and our greeting meeting was scheduled for 7:00 pm. There would be around a thousand people there. Amy was nervous too, but was hiding it better than me. I had done enough travelling to be rather jaded and I knew we would have no time to see the city. We had three days and they were all scheduled. Still, I smiled as I watched Amy be mesmerized by the city, taking pictures as we walked down a street. I felt my phone vibrate in my pocket. I took it out and saw I had a woof from someone called J.B. I looked at his profile and was blown away. He was twenty-six and was possibly the most handsome man I had ever seen, rivalling even Adam, who was gone but not forgotten. *Hey, handsome welcome to my city. Want to hang out?* his message read.

"Amy, AMY! Look at this guy." I shouted at her.

"What?" she asked

"Look, LOOK!"

She looked at my phone. "Yeah, I guess," she shrugged.

"What do I do?' I asked

"Message him back. He is probably only after sex but he looks sweet." "What do I say?"

After considering it for a few minutes I said what I was feeling. *J.B. thank you so much, you have made my week. I am flattered that someone as handsome and sweet as you would message me. I am only here for a few days but if I get a chance to hang out you will be the first to know.*

He responded a simple word: *Cool.*

I was all over the place. More woofs and messages were coming in and these American boys were hot as hell, polite and charming but J.B. resonated with me as I walked into my hotel room and was greeted by three Squad roommates. I was getting excited and a little emotional.

"Guys, I've never thought of myself as sexually attractive and these men are saying I am. Even if they only want sex, I'm okay with that. I don't care if that is right or wrong."

I was processing my thoughts verbally and I was feeling sexy for the first time in my life.

"You are sexy," Malcolm, our Squad leader said. "This is a new opportunity for you. Embrace it."

Being able to share with these people what was going on was a gift and the support they were giving me made me feel secure enough to be open to the possibility that I had something to offer.

That night, Amy and I were having a late dinner and I began to cry at the table. "Amy, I really thought I had missed this. Missed being young and sexy and having men finding me attractive. I feel so lucky. Thank you for encouraging me to do this."

Thinking back to the Beast and the hangar and that day I wanted to end it all, I saw that I would have never known that I had sex appeal; I committed to Amy that I would own this part of me. Over the weekend, I messaged other men and communicated with them as I had with J.B., with openness and kindness. I got very little sleep.

Nothing at all happened over the weekend with any of my new text buddies but it allowed me to embrace myself in a totally new way: it went against everything I had ever believed about my appearance and my body. None of it was wrong, and I was thrilled with myself for doing this, for the people around me supporting me. Most of all, I was and am grateful to J.B. from Minneapolis. Thank you for that woof and a whole lot more.

24

The list and the make-up bag

Returning to Vancouver, I finally got to meet Cheeky Chappy. Not being a total newbie, I bought condoms and lube in my local Safeway store to be prepared for whatever came next. Chappy and I went for noodles and he impressed me immediately with his car. It was very odd meeting someone for the first time after texting and sharing graphic pictures with each other. He was a nice guy, very relaxing, with a glint in his eyes. After dinner, he drove me home and I asked him in for a cup of tea and ice cream. We both knew what the intention was but I really did have ice cream, a tub of Chunky Monkey and chocolate, in case he was the more traditional sort. After the tea and ice cream on the couch, we got to that moment.

"I am probably rusty as hell," I admitted as I gazed into his blue eyes.

"Me too," he claimed.

No mate, I am as totally rusty as can be.

I leaned in and we started kissing and that led to other things. I showed him the condoms and he looked dubious.

"What?" I asked.

"You may need another brand." Then he saw the lube.

"Where did you get this?"

"Safeway."

"You really are rusty, aren't you?"

"That is what I've been saying for the last few hours."

"It's okay. You're lucky you are cute," Chappy said.

He asked for a piece of paper and a pen and wrote me a shopping list. "You need to go to a sex shop and pick up these items."

"Okay, but why do I need them?" I asked

He explained it to me for the next hour or as we got up to other things.

"Thank you for making this fun," I told him at the end of the night.

The next day I fulfilled my promise and found myself in a sex shop on Davie Street. I went straight to the girl at the desk and took out my shopping list. I had a flashback to my childhood when Dean and I would go shopping for his mother. She wrote lists but not one like this. The condoms were easy enough to find, with the gun-like name of Magnum. I felt like a badass picking them up. Then came the lube: this was a real education. I was chatting to this girl about it like it was a household cleaner.

"Does your boyfriend get an irritable bum?" she asked.

Feeling very brave, I answered, "I am not familiar enough with his bum yet to know."

She laughed out loud. "Right. Well, this is the best and safest brand. I use it myself."

That was high praise. I took a photo to prove to Cheeky Chappy that I had achieved my objective. He congratulated me and I felt like I had just been given a gold star.

Chappy wasn't the only man after me, however. I am cautious of young guys, if only not to be seen as a cradle snatcher. But one guy, Man on a Mission, had been messaging me and asking for a date and I accepted for the following night. I had a full day teaching and I wasn't that eager to have a dinner date in Gastown that night but there I was. Mission was a nice guy, sweet and innocent looking. By 10:30 pm, I tried to leave and get home.

"I've come from Surrey, so can I at least walk you home?" he asked.

"Isn't that out of your way?"

"No," he said.

On the Skytrain, he insisted on coming into my place for a cup of tea. I couldn't shake him. I made him tea and even gave him some cookies, which reminded me he was only twenty-two, a mere child in my eyes. I sat on the couch beside him with a large space between us. He finished his tea and looked at me.

"Ok, I don't know what to do or say next," I admitted. "What do you want?"

"I want to have sex with you," he said, as calm as anything.

"Okay, well, I may have had sex earlier and I may have sex tomorrow with someone else. Are you okay with that?"

"You are cute," he answered. "Now take off your clothes."

I complied with his request figuring he was in charge for the next little while. The old me wouldn't have let this happen. I would have gotten all caught up with the morality and age issues. But what the hell. After he had his way with me, I walked him to the Skytrain.

"Thank you for tonight," I said. "You made me feel young."

"Sure, thanks," Mission said, as the train door closed. I never heard from him again.

I talked to Dr. Ed about all this as I was still seeing him but now on a monthly basis. He agreed that I should keep getting out there. I was shocked.

"Really?" I asked him

"Yes. You need to explore this and talking about it isn't enough. You are responsible and you have my number and remember—if you don't feel safe, don't do it."

That blew my mind. If my therapist was supporting this action, then I was going to continue. Besides, this was my choice and my life and I wanted to keep going and exploring. People began to notice a huge shift in me. I was smiling and happy. I was giddy. I was having a great time, totally free of anything or anyone getting in my way. This was my time, finally—my turn to live, and beautifully. I was surprising myself too; I got nothing but support from Amy and friends around me. Zara, in particular, was thrilled I was now getting pole.

Poor Ben was more in shock. He sat on the couch repeating, "What have I created?"

"A raging sex beast," I told him. "Aren't you proud?"

"No, I'm actually a little scared."

Now that made me smile.

"Who is the dirty little whore now?" he asked.

I raised my hand in acknowledgement and gave him his tea.

Walking around with a backpack full of condoms and lube is never a good idea as I discovered over lunch while meeting a Cornerstone friend I hadn't seen in a few months. She had pushed me hard over the past year to get back into the dating scene and I was excited to see her. "You were so right! Getting out there was the only thing to do. I have met so many different types of men and I am having so much fun," I told her.

Going to my bag to pull out a card I had bought her to say thank you for all her support, a condom came flying out instead. It landed on the ground beside us. I sheepishly put my hand out to grab it.

"Woops." People around us glared.

"Robert! Do you not have a bag for them?" my friend asked.

"No."

She pulled out a small make-up bag from her own handbag and emptied the contents. She handed it to me and said, "Here, put them in this. The lube too."

I felt like I was being given a trophy of sorts. I was now officially a sexual being, an adult man fully prepared for adult encounters.

I showed Amy and Ben my new bag the next Friday when I

had them both over for dinner. While eating, I was messaged by a visiting man called Traveler and I was only half looking at his messages. He suggested coffee the next day and I agreed to meet him for lunch.

I was half expecting him not to turn up when I entered the coffee shop, but bought myself a coffee and waited. He arrived and, to my surprise, was very attractive and wore glasses, always a plus in my book. We sat and talked for a few hours. He was an amazingly accomplished individual from overseas, in Vancouver for a conference. He wasn't out as it wasn't an option for him; my heart went out to him because I knew what he was hiding and the cost of doing so. As we talked I found myself feeling something for him.

"So, what do you want to do now?" Traveler asked.

"I'm easy," I said.

"Well, we can go upstairs if you like or we can go for a walk."

Sod walking. I do that every day. But I gave him my developing honest, direct answer.

"Look, I am here for you. Whatever you want to do." I said.

I meant it too. I wanted to be of service to him. I couldn't change his world but right now I could be there for him.

"I'd like to go upstairs," he admitted.

Phew, after the gym, my legs are killing me.

His room had a great view. He was nervous and so was I. The gentleness of the whole encounter stuck with me and, as things progressed, Traveler stopped and said, "I don't have any lube."

"Not a problem," I said, reaching for my backpack.

I pulled out my bag and was thrilled to be able to share the story of how I had gotten it with him. I opened it up and pulled out the contents.

"You come prepared," he said.

Afterwards, as we were parting ways, I gave him my email

address. I had never done this before but I said, "If you ever need to reach out, here is my email."

I left the hotel feeling ten feet tall. This wasn't just about my physical gratification, it was about who I could be for other people. I was choosing to be loving and caring for someone I would have liked to know better had we lived in the same world.

There were downsides to all this playing around. I didn't always get it right and had to deal with a potential stalker; being responsible also meant getting blood work and STI checks done to make sure I wasn't carrying anything. The hardest thing was not getting attached. I felt attached to Cheeky Chappy and that was difficult to let go of in the beginning.

I didn't have much expectation of finding my future husband in this way but that wasn't the goal. I was still learning and I suppose the scariest thing for me was getting injured through all this activity. I was balancing Cornerstone commitments and it was a challenge; I had volunteered to coach on an upcoming course and was out with a guy the night before. We were busy most of the night and I limped home feeling exhausted and a little tender in my nether regions. Going to take a pee, I noticed my poor member was swollen and very tender.

Oh my God! What have I done?

I had once caught my foreskin in my zipper and this brought all that fear flooding back. I was coaching the next day, so I decided not to panic as there was no blood or anything like that. I left myself alone and prayed that by morning it would be better. I really didn't want to make that call to Cornerstone. Saying I was sick wouldn't cut it as an excuse not to turn up. Could I say, "Hi, this is Rob. I can't coach today because my penis is swollen."

Having a cup of warm milk before bed, I had to soothe myself: *You choose to play around tonight and it was fun and you got a bit injured. Let's not let that happen again. If we have to make* that phone call in the morning, then you can and will make it. Let them decide what to do. The Beast in the hangar flashed into my head. That is why I was here in Vancouver. That is why I was doing all this exploration. I was doing this to be a better man, a grown, confident, sexually secure man.

I slept well that night and the next morning my penis was back to normal. It was still tender but the swelling was gone and I went into coach.

25

It's all about the technique

Throughout all this change and excitement, I was still being confronted by my speech. It was woven deep into my psyche and I still feared it. Being a late bloomer, I could be gentle and give myself the permission to explore my sexuality and laugh at myself when I got it wrong. I couldn't do this with my speech, even with all the therapy and techniques. Squad was to confront this side of me, which I knew from the minute I signed up. Having to speak in groups, take on coaching and leadership and, most of all, use the phone to make calls. The phone was still a huge trigger for me and, without my McGuire support, I felt alone and misunderstood.

Giving myself permission to use McGuire technique in the outside world was challenging. I know this because I had an opportunity to speak via Skype to many old friends back home in Dublin on National Stammering Awareness Day, October 22, 2016. Michael, a master graduate and someone I respected, had asked me if I would be willing to talk as he knew my story and wanted to highlight the growing area of study looking at the emotional similarities of coming out as gay and coming out as a recovering stutterer. Having been through both, I could confirm that there were emotional similarities. Every time I have come out to someone regarding my speech or sexuality, there is a cost to me, along with the ever-present fear of being rejected or judged.

But put me in a room with recovering McGuire graduates and my technique will be strong as it was on that October day when I found myself on Skype talking to a ballroom full of stutterers and speech therapists. My technique was controlled and comfortable. I spoke for fifteen minutes, off the cuff, about my story, suicide attempt, and the ramifications. I focused on things like vulnerability, authenticity and playing big in life. All things that sounded very insightful coming out of my mouth, yet I was not able to follow my own advice.

Cornerstone worked on a totally different principle. I was told I could disappear my stutter by speaking from nothing. I could imagine speaking from nothing as meaning speaking without fear or holding back. Yet, I hadn't spoken like that for over thirty years and I didn't really believe I could disappear my stutter. More to the point, I wasn't sure I wanted to: I was that attached to it. Either way, I had committed to working in the Cornerstone offices three hours a week and that meant a lot of phone calls to people interested in the courses and following up with people who had already signed up. Trying to breathe and stay calm was impossible and it took all my courage to keep dialing. I hoped that, eventually, I would find a way to relax, to let go of my fear and embarrassment, while throwing in some technique.

"As you practice more, you will get better at this," Kayla, one of the senior coaches, told me. That was fine, assuming I survived the process. I was coaching for the first time on her course the day after I injured my penis and I wanted to support her even though I didn't feel qualified or experienced enough to coach. My mind was racing with questions.

What if my speech fails me on stage when I am doing my coaching pitch to the room? Followed by: *What if I can't coach properly on the phone because of my speech?*

I sat in the room twisting myself into knots. I wished someone from the McGuire Programme was there with me. They would get the fear and have some sound advice for me, something like use a little basic technique to relax and just have fun. Everyone kept telling me to have fun. In these situations, I never felt like having fun. It felt like a performance, like acting, and I was anxious. When it came to my turn to pitch myself as a coach, I tried to say something inspiring.

"I am a stand for each of you to own your own power, powerfully. I was sitting where you are now six months ago and I fought it and questioned everything. So if you are in the same situation, I am the coach for you."

Bingo. It will be like the blind leading the blind. Poor eejits have no idea what they are letting themselves in for.

I ended up with four students, including a handsome, successful man. When he came towards me, I felt a mixture of excitement, bewilderment and sheer panic. The three other students were women and that was much less daunting. We all went to dinner where I explained how the coaching worked and that we would be in communication for fifteen minutes daily over the next week. There were forms to fill in and that allowed me to fill the time: name, phone number, what they wanted to achieve over the week. I fell back on my teacher training and managed to sound like I knew what I was doing.

Over the week, I coached as instructed, but my speech was being triggered by everything. I felt all these emotions and was shocking. On one of the coaches' group calls, I tried to tell Kayla that I was struggling.

"Kayla, this is em-em-em-em R-R-Rob. I am h-h-having an issue around t-t-this point."

I felt shame and embarrassment and anger, but not like in the past. I wasn't being consumed by them. Well, at least now everyone knows I stutter and I am not just making it up. I was validating my own story. *See! This is me coming from nothing, people!*

Kayla dealt with my issue in rapid fashion and told me again to come from nothing in my speech. I thanked her and, twenty minutes after I hung up the phone, I got a call from my Squad team leader. She was checking in on me. I thanked her for calling me. I told her everything I knew to say.

"I am fine. This is where I knew I would be and this is a breakdown. I am giving up feeling embarrassed and ashamed and I am committed to working on this and being a great coach and a powerful leader."

I meant every word. I was feeling stupid and exposed, but the anger and rage that would have been there in the past were gone. I could sit with my feelings on the matter and that was yet another transformation. That night, though, I couldn't sleep. I felt the familiar panic begin to rise. *How the hell can I come from nothing?*

Then it hit me. Use technique. I saw that I was making the whole McGuire Programme wrong. I told myself that they were freaks and I sounded like a freak when I used technique. Yet, as a graduate, I knew various tools to use on the phone to get over my fear. I had used them on my Skype call to Ireland just recently. Could technique allow me to come from nothing? What if I didn't care how I sounded? Would that give me the freedom I needed? I looked at my life in Vancouver and saw so clearly that it wasn't working. I had never acted due to my fear of stuttering. I was scared to change jobs because of my stutter. I was afraid to step into my own power because of stuttering. The coaching call had been a disaster because of my fear of stuttering. And then the other shoe dropped.

I was stopping myself from using technique because I told myself crap, such as I sound like a freak. I was making everyone wrong—Cornerstone, McGuire, Kayla, all of them. I wanted to be a stutterer to stay small, single and sad. I knew the technique but I chose not to use it.

I had always been aware of my resistance but, in that moment, I got that I was choosing this. A little bit of technique at the beginning of the coaching call would have put me at ease, but I was still trying to play the role of a fluent speaker and failing. I was still avoiding living big because at some point I would have to own up to my stuttering nature. Could Cornerstone make it disappear? It really didn't matter. I wanted to be free from the fear of it. The technique was my ticket out of this trap. To bring it into my everyday speaking, to play with it like I was doing with the dating would take commitment and love towards myself. I had begun to like myself, but loving myself? Stutter and all?

It was now 4:30 am and I tried to call my McGuire coaches and friends. I reached Michael and told him, "I have been making you and the Programme wrong. I am a hypocrite and fraud and I am not going to do that anymore. I spoke to a room full of stutterers, was judging them as being inferior to me, when I am nowhere near as self-actualized as they are. I am miserable and small and I am the one doing that to myself. I am going to commit to taking action, to actively using the technique every day and bring it into my speaking."

Michael thanked me for being honest and I felt I finally understood. It wasn't the stutter keeping me small. It was me using the stutter to keep myself small.

By 6:00 am, I finally dozed off and got a few hours' sleep. I felt tired throughout the day but energized too. It was the final night of Kayla's course and before we began, I stood up and told the room, "Thank you for the call last night. It was perfect. I am committed to using my technique to control my speech and not let that happen again. I am here to stand for my students and you guys, especially you, Kayla, and I am taking this on fully. I am tired of playing small. I discovered I was making the McGuire Programme and you wrong when I am the one making myself wrong. I am cleaning that up."

The group erupted into applause. I felt so complete in that

moment. I was a stuttering homosexual and his race car was in a hangar thousands of miles away, waiting. Waiting for me to reach this point; to be the man I was always meant to be. There was no fear or blame or anger; rather serenity and the exciting question of what was coming next. A stark contrast to how I felt in the hangar the day I tried to kill myself; I knew from here on, everything would be different. Not easy, but different because I was choosing to change and to do what I knew to do. Not for anyone other than myself. And, maybe, for a black racing car too.

26

Owning the story

My story, the true story of a stuttering homosexual and his race car, is one I created. I believed I was broken. I believed I was inferior and I believed I deserved to suffer. Being fixed, passing as "normal"—whatever that is—and trying to fit in was something I was so committed to that I was like a hamster on a wheel. Running all the time. I never saw life as fun or exciting and, as I grew older, I didn't want to let go of the story as it was all I thought I had. The attachment I felt was so deep and it felt so real that now, as that story ends and a new one begins, I find myself in a wonderful space of transition. Transition to create a new story, a better story full of joy and excitement and—most of all—love. But to do that means really letting go of the old one. All the pain and sorrow for wasted time.

Being gay may not have been my choice, but the way I relate to it is. I can fight it and make it wrong or decide to accept it. My stutter will always be there too, but does it need to be an enemy? Do I need to rigidly control it? Not anymore. It is a part of me and it is not the disempowering defect I have always seen it as. It is the piece of me that ran in fear from the world, but now I see it as the access to my vulnerability. While it takes courage to expose myself as a stutterer, doing so allows others to be vulnerable with me as well; that is when the magic of connection truly happens.

The end of this story is the beginning of this story: who I am and who I have always been. Robert, the boy who loved cars, transforming alien robots and starships. The boy who didn't know fear and judgement. The boy who was free to be himself. On this journey, there has always been a car: the Beast. It supported me and motivated me without ever turning a wheel. The passion I feel for it and the dream of many more drives is what keeps me standing strong because I may falter and fail but I will never give up on it. It is a piece of me, just like my sexuality and speech. I've earned the right to be me—a geeky car fanatic with a personal relationship with his vehicles.

I am not wrong. I am not broken.

We have the right to craft our lives, write our own stories and live our lives fully, for no one other than ourselves because the truth is, no one else can.

Prologue: Sunday, July 14, 2019

Ballygarrett, County Wexford: the clock reads 5:00 am. I haven't slept more than two hours but still feel wired from the day before. The gentle snoring coming from my new husband in the bed beside me tells me he is still sleeping. I inch myself off the mattress, quietly putting on a pair of jeans and a T-shirt that are sitting on top of my rucksack. I walk around the bed and leave a note beside his pillow: *Gone for a drive. Sleep tight. X.* My driving shoes are at the foot of the bed; I grab them on the way out and head toward the kitchen.

Mum and Dad's house in Ballygarrett has never been so full. We have two full families in residence and a few straggling guests on couches. The kitchen is empty and it is still dark outside. I boil the kettle and go to eat some of the leftovers from the day before. Cold turkey on bread has never tasted so amazing. I grab a small piece of cake as dessert. I'll hit the gym next week. Lemon sponge wasn't my first choice but it had a surprising tang that makes me smile. I got to choose the wedding venue, so he got to choose the food.

The sun is slowly rising now and the day is beginning. I grab the keys hanging on the key rack and quietly open the back door, locking it again as I go. It is not necessary but old habits die hard— Dad is a stickler for these kinds of things. I walk down the garden path and in front of me is the hangar with the wedding tent still standing beside it. The marquee will be collected later today along with the tables and chairs. Dad put up lights and hired a local band to play well into the night, but no one complained about the noise, the house and hangar being located on a seven-acre site. Besides, the whole village of Ballygarrett had come to my wedding, along with our families and friends. Faint wafts of stale beer linger in the air. I'd had two glasses of wine but nothing more; having a promise to keep this morning, I hadn't wanted to be groggy or tired.

I walk to the hangar door and unlock it. Over the last year or two, Dad has cleared out most of the junk. Switching on the lights, I see 98-D-1333 in its new space under the mezzanine platform. The car is now more than twenty years old, and I spent the last year stripping and rebuilding it. Sitting idle had taken its toll on my car. The engine needed very little work but many of the ancillaries had degraded. The new gearbox and steering rack have been slightly modified to give it a firmer, more sporting personality. I had toyed with the idea of fitting the later Polo GTI running gear but, in the end, I wanted it to remain as original as possible. It was no longer my daily drive but a hobbyist vehicle. I had begun my racing license training in it and just couldn't bring myself to sell it.

Beside the Polo was Dad's tractor, which he uses to cut the grass on a weekly basis—a seven-acre site needs a lot of attention. Dad moans about endlessly but I know he loves playing "Farmer Jim" and it keeps him out of Mum's hair too, so everyone wins. Dad's E38 Seven series is next in the line of vehicles. Covered and charging. The E38 hasn't reached classic status yet but, like the Polo for me, the Seven has more sentimental value for Dad than anything else. Since the hangar is massive, space is not an issue. I haven't come for any of these cars though.

Sitting in front of them all is the M3. The red wedding ribbons are still attached to the car. I didn't dare disappear after the ceremony to tend to such a trivial thing but now I carefully remove them, starting from the front of the bonnet. I fold the ribbon and put it in the M3's storage area. I'm really getting sentimental in my old age, aren't I, old friend?

Running my hand along the bonnet, I know the engine

underneath has been fully serviced and is ready for the road trip to Germany and the Nürburgring next month as part of my extended honeymoon. This trip has been in the planning for months and we will have a support car following us. Dad complained about having to get a racing license, but those are the rules.

The Beast smells as it has always smelled: a curious mix of old plastic, oil and petrol. The aroma takes me back to my childhood so easily, and I hope the smell will remain after the scheduled rebuild when our track adventure is over. The experience and contacts I made during 98-D-1333's rebuild encouraged me to consider rebuilding the Beast back to its factory specification. I leveraged BMW itself to take on the task, as they have a special classic division that deals with such things. The success of my book and the publicity that it attracted has helped. The rebuild will take at least six months.

But that is the future. Right now, I admire the newly recovered and reattached Alcantara suede steering wheel, a wedding present from Dad. My wedding band feels funny against the material as I don't normally wear rings, but this one I wear with pride.

I start the engine and it erupts into life, shaking the car as it has always done. I look at my wedding ring again.

"Thank you," I whisper to the car.

How different everything is now, even though the view is the same as the one I saw on that day of despair. The promise of just one more drive, in this car, on a morning like this, was enough to keep me fighting. I know that now. I know that I saved myself and I know that I am loved and I know that it was the promise of this day and this drive that kept me fighting for myself; when I wasn't strong enough to do that, I fought for the M3.

I open the hangar door and the morning sunlight streams in. I inch the car out slowly and wait as the doors close behind us. There is dew evaporating on the grass and, although it is still chilly outside, inside the car is warm. The seat is hugging me tight and I feel safe and comfortable. This is where I belong. The clock reads 5:47 am and I drive away as quietly as possible.

The village is still sleeping and the roads are deserted. I let the car fully warm up and, as the oil and water temperature gauges settle into their optimal position, I slowly begin to dance with the Beast. After months of lessons, I am intimately familiar with this car now. Every pitch, every sound and every sensation under me. But this isn't a race. This is a Sunday morning drive. This is our victory lap.

I drive along the coast road heading for the Wicklow mountains. After about an hour, we're at Glendalough. I haven't been here since I was a teenager and I marvel at the beauty of the place. I pull the car over and get out. It's nearly 7:00 am and I put on my jacket. I walk towards the edge of the road and can see a lake in the distance. The air is fresh and crisp and wipes away any hint of fatigue. The M3 is binging and creaking beside me as it cools in the morning air.

As I stand and look out at the lake I can't help but feel a little emotional. Over the last two years, everything has changed for me. I never thought I would see forty. That milestone year had been terrifying but it was also the year I fell in love. It was the year I launched my book and it was the year I left Vancouver to begin my life anew. My home will be wherever he is. We have talked about living in Vancouver and Ireland, but nothing has been decided yet. To my joy, he wants kids. Being a few years older than him, I am apprehensive but willing to embrace the possibility. This is all I have always wanted: to love and be loved.

I look back at the M3 and smile. Seeing it now, here, makes me beam with pride. The Beast was the catalyst; it was the rock, the motivator I needed. It saved me and now I was saving it. I say a prayer for Dan and think of him as I look on across the horizon. I no longer envy him but I do understand his decision; that is why I wrote this book. Not for money, or for fame. But for Dan, for my fourteen-year-old self and for anyone else who is lost and hurting. What began as a private death diary has become a celebration of life, of hope and of faith.

My phone vibrates in my pocket. I take it out; 7:10 am and I have a text message.

Where are you? I got your note but didn't think you were serious about going for a drive at this hour.

I'm at Glendalough, I text back. *Don't worry, all is good. I just wanted to stretch the M3's legs.*

Well, when you are finished cheating on me with the real love of your life, can you get yourself home. Breakfast is at 9:00 am and I think I can hear your mother shuffling around downstairs.

Mum never could sleep.

I'll be home soon and I love you, I text back

I love you too, you adorable freak. Drive safely.

I put my phone back into my pocket and get back into the Beast. Today I am a married man. I smile. The M3 had kept the dream alive by keeping the dreamer alive and safe. I may be older and a little wiser but, in my heart, I am still just a boy sitting in a car waiting for the next adventure to begin. I turn the key and reverse.

"Let's go home," I say to the M3, and we head out for one more drive.